David Brock and
Paul Waldman
Free Ride

David Brock is the author of four political books,
including *The Republican Noise Machine: Right-Wing
Media and How It Corrupts Democracy*. In his preced-
ing book, *Blinded by the Right: The Conscience of an
Ex-Conservative*, a 2002 *New York Times* bestselling
political memoir, he chronicled his years as a conservative media insider.

Paul Waldman is the author or coauthor of three
books on politics and media, including *The Press
Effect: Politicians, Journalists, and the Stories That Shape
the Political World*. His last book was *Being Right
Is Not Enough: What Progressives Must Learn From
Conservative Success*. He is also a columnist for *The
American Prospect*.

Free Ride

John McCain and the Media

**David Brock and
Paul Waldman**

ANCHOR BOOKS

A Division of Random House, Inc.

New York

An Anchor Books Original, April 2008

Copyright © 2008 by David Brock and Paul Waldman

All rights reserved. Published in the United States by Anchor Books,
a division of Random House, Inc., New York, and in Canada by
Random House of Canada Limited, Toronto.

Anchor Books and colophon are registered trademarks of Random House, Inc.

Library of Congress Cataloging-in-Publication Data
Brock, David, 1962–
Free Ride/David Brock and Paul Waldman.
p. cm.
Includes bibliographical references.
ISBN 978-0-307-27940-8
1. McCain, John, 1936– 2. United States—Politics and government—2001–
3. Presidential candidates—United States—Biography. 4. Press and politics—
United States. 5. Mass media—Political aspects—United States.
6. Legislators—United States—Biography. 7. United States. Congress. Senate—
Biography.
I. Title.
E840.8.M26B76 2008
328.73'092—dc22
[B] 2007049763

Book design by Debbie Glasserman

www.anchorbooks.com

Printed in the United States of America
10 9 8 7 6 5 4 3

Contents

Foreword
The Myth of McCain

Over the course of a career, most nationally prominent politicians, particularly those who choose to seek the White House, can expect ups and downs in their treatment by the press. While some are looked on more favorably than others, most of the key figures in national politics will see times when they are hailed as victors and praised for their strengths, and times when they are derided as losers and pilloried for their weaknesses. But in recent years, there has been one exception to this rule: John McCain. While other politicians are examined with a cynical eye, McCain and his admirers in the media have cooperated to construct a shimmering image of the senator from Arizona, one that has propelled him to the heights of American politics. McCain, as he has been presented to the public, is a straight-talking maverick, a war hero standing astride the parties and untroubled by political calculations.

As the forthcoming chapters will show, no other modern politician has received as much favorable press as John McCain has in the past decade, a period that has seen him go from a relative unknown to the man that *The Almanac of American Politics* calls "the closest thing our politics has to a national hero."[1] While some politicians might get nearly as much attention, and a few others (such as Chuck Hagel or Richard Lugar) are privileged with steadily laudatory press, McCain stands alone in the combination of his high profile in the media and the overwhelmingly positive tone of the coverage that the press gives him.

But calling McCain's coverage positive does not begin to convey the complexity of his singular status in the media. In a hundred ways, the rules are simply different for McCain. Indeed, when writing about McCain, journalists offer a unique brand of praise. Here are a few of the things hard-bitten reporters said about McCain during his 2000 run for the presidency:

- "A man of unshakable character, willing to stand up for his convictions."[2] (R. W. Apple, *New York Times*)
- "An original, imaginative, and at times inspiring candidate."[3] (Jacob Weisberg, *Slate*)
- "Mr. McCain is running as the blunt anti-politician who won't lie, who won't spin."[4] (Alison Mitchell, *New York Times*)
- "While most candidates talk up their chances, McCain engages in anti-spin."[5] (Howard Kurtz, *Washington Post*)
- "He rises above the pack in admitting it's not all the other party's fault. He's eloquent, as only a prisoner of war can be."[6] (David Nyhan, *Boston Globe*)

- "McCain conveys a great sense of vigor, a sense that anything can happen on his campaign."[7] (Roger Simon, *U.S. News & World Report*)
- "There's something authentic about this man."[8] (Mike Wallace, *60 Minutes*)
- "Basically just a cool dude."[9] (Jake Tapper, *Salon*)

This sampling—all from the campaign season, when reporters tend to be *more* cynical—only skims the surface. In story after story, the media portrayed—and continue to portray—John McCain as a larger-than-life anti-politician, unbeholden to special interests and driven not by ambition but by a sense of duty. Such was the rapport that developed between McCain and the media in 2000 that McCain staffers began to call the media their "base." As Michael Lewis, a frequent magazine contributor and bestselling author, wrote about McCain in 1997, "I became used to opening the morning paper and finding McCain's quotes on the front page and his opinions echoed on the editorial page. It was a testament to the growing distrust between the press and the more ordinary politicians. Here was a Republican Senator—a red meat, pro-life, strong-army kind of guy—and yet somehow he had become the preferred source of the putatively liberal media."[10]

Lewis may have been one of the first reporters to turn his wordsmithing talents to the elevation of John McCain the politician (R. W. Apple also wrote some of the first tributes to McCain, in the *New York Times*), but he was hardly the last. David Broder and David Ignatius of the *Washington Post*, Howard Fineman of *Newsweek*, Joe Klein of *Time* (who described McCain's 2000 campaign as containing "hints of what politics might become . . . if we're lucky"[11]), and Chris Matthews of MSNBC would have to be counted among McCain's most enthusiastic current boosters in the major media. Although these men may be more demonstrative in their admiration for McCain, that admiration is evident in nearly all the coverage McCain has received, particularly since his campaign for the 2000 Republican nomination for president.

The result has been a virtually indestructible media creation: the Myth of McCain. We call it a "myth" not to assert that all the themes that run through the coverage of McCain are plainly false. Rather, we use the term according to its dictionary definition, meaning the foundational set of precepts on which a belief system is based. Even as his 2008 campaign experienced some early stumbles and he did things that seemed to call into question the foundations of his image, the Myth of McCain remained intact. The myth consists of the following ideas:

- John McCain is a maverick.
- John McCain is a moderate.
- John McCain is a straight talker.
- John McCain is a reformer.
- John McCain doesn't do things just because they're politically expedient.
- Just about all you need to know about John McCain's character is that he showed courage as a prisoner of war in Vietnam.
- John McCain has too much integrity to use his war record to his political advantage.

Some of these ideas have a basis in reality but have been wildly exaggerated; others are simply false. What is incontrovertible is that the press has continually foregrounded them at the expense of a more rounded and accurate portrait of McCain.

Even when early problems on the 2008 campaign trail (such as lackluster fund-raising in the first quarter of 2007) resulted in some uncharacteristically critical coverage for McCain, the elements of the myth remained intact. What that period of more critical press showed was that even McCain's negative coverage is more positive than that which other candidates receive. Unlike other candidates, McCain finds that momentary controversies (as when he responded to a question about Iran by singing "Bomb bomb bomb, bomb bomb Iran" to the tune of "Barbara Ann") are presented in isolation, unconnected to any alleged character flaws.

The contrast with other candidates is striking. When Mitt Romney makes a seemingly exaggerated claim about his history as a hunter, reporters connect the statement to doubts about whether Romney is genuine and sincere. When John Edwards gets an expensive haircut, reporters question whether he is a true populist and sufficiently substantive. The allegedly revealing incidents are contextualized by other similar incidents from the candidate's past and then brought up again and again in the future. In other words, the negative press of the moment is linked to what we are told are the candidates' significant flaws, the deficiencies in their character that "raise questions" about whether they are fit to be president.

Not so for John McCain. The very idea that McCain might have deficiencies of character that relate to his fitness to be president is never contemplated. The consequence is that a spate of bad coverage, whether over a temporarily struggling campaign or an intemperate remark, does nothing to undermine his prospects for a future comeback. Others find their worst moments replayed over and over, used to indict their character and highlight their flaws. But the John McCain portrayed in the media has no character flaws. He may say something dumb or be down in the polls, but his fundamental virtue is never questioned. If he is down, he is therefore always poised for a revival. If he panders, he will resume his admirable candor any day—as an April 2007 column by David Broder of the *Washington Post* was titled, he'll be "Straight Talking Again."[12] In an editorial two days later, Broder's newspaper wrote, "Whatever your position on the war, then or now, Mr. McCain deserves credit for foresight and consistency about how the war should have been waged . . . the 2008 race is better for having Mr. McCain in it."[13] Even a flagging campaign can be presented as evidence of McCain's fundamental goodness; noting that McCain seemed "dispirited" in early 2007, *Newsweek* offered, "It may be because he is not, at heart, a politician. He is a warrior."[14] When a reporter says someone is "not a politician," it is the highest compliment (and exceedingly odd if the man in question has been a politician for a quarter of a century).

Over his career, McCain has compiled a record that is far more complex than his media image. The fact of the matter is that John McCain is neither a moderate nor a maverick. McCain's voting record, his ideas, his values, and his rhetoric mark him as a stout conservative—a description that he himself adheres to. And despite occasional acts of seeming apostasy, McCain has actually been a dependably loyal member of the Republican Party. A close examination of the occasions on which he does break with the GOP—as on campaign finance reform, for instance—reveals them to be not just carefully calculated, but both less substantively meaningful and less risky than the way they are portrayed in the media.

By reading heroic qualities in every facet of the Arizona senator, the media have failed to give the public an accurate portrait of McCain the politician. For here is a man who, in the end, is not much different from his colleagues in Congress in ambition, calculation, and attraction to power. John McCain has been in politics for twenty-five years now. He is currently in his fourth Senate term. He has been a major contender for the presidency and is one of the most visible legislators in recent history. An anti-politician he is not.

Yet McCain is distinct from his colleagues in some critical ways. More so than any other contemporary political figure, he has cracked the media code. His careful courting of the press has resulted in the very picture of him that most serves his ends, where every statement uttered, every position taken, even every external event seems to be characterized only in the way most compli-mentary to John McCain. He has obtained what every politician yearns for: a press corps that acts almost as a partner in his polit-ical ambitions.

The fawning coverage has barely abated even as McCain has made a very public hard tack to the right in preparing for his sec-ond run at the presidency. In an effort to win support among the Republican Party's conservative base, without which it will be nearly impossible for him to win the party's nomination for presi-dent, McCain has sought to be more vocal and demonstrative about his genuine conservatism—a conservatism that, running in 2000 against the establishment candidate, George W. Bush, he was happy to see obscured as he made an effort to attract moderates. Despite such a shift, the media have continued to champion McCain as a moderate among ideologues and the straightest of straight talkers.

And though in late 2006 and early 2007 McCain did receive some unfavorable coverage as his campaign seemed to have trouble getting off the ground, the old affection was evident in a press corps seemingly eager for McCain to reignite the spirit of his 2000 run. "John McCain is back on the bus," proclaimed ABC's *Nightline* in March 2007. "And everywhere he goes, McCain takes on all comers, all questions. A rolling no-holds-barred polit-ical free-for-all, unlike most other American campaigns these days." When McCain said he had no choice but to do what's right, correspondent Terry Moran commented, "No other choice. That's pure John McCain. Blunt, unyielding, deploying his principles . . . What he does do is what he's always done, play it as straight as pos-sible . . . The maverick candidate still. John McCain."[15]

If tributes like that one were rarer on the 2008 campaign trail than they had been in the past, their continued presence high-lighted the unique relationship between McCain and the media, a phenomenon that simply finds no comparison in modern politics. It is important to understand the phenomenon simply because of who McCain is. As one of the leading candidates for the presi-dency in 2008, John McCain stands as one of the most important figures on the American political landscape. Is the McCain that the media are giving us the McCain we're actually getting? Are the media covering McCain comprehensively, accurately, and thought-fully—qualities that we seek in all reportage on our leaders?

But the question of how the media cover McCain has larger implications that go beyond 2008. For the last three or four decades, the media have stood as the single most important insti-tution in American electoral politics. It is the media, more than the parties (or, arguably, even the candidates themselves), that define the pictures that voters carry in their heads as they walk into the voting booth. The media's complicity in the canonization of John McCain is an object lesson in their failure to serve the American public.

Throughout this book we refer alternately to "the media," "the press," "reporters," or "journalists." It is important to understand that the contemporary American news media form an enormously complex organism. National politicians like John McCain are presented to the public in a variety of ways and through a variety of voices. What concerns us most is the overall picture, the image that accumulates over thousands of news stories and television appearances, through repeated tropes and unspoken premises. This portrait is created by individual people making individual decisions. No one understands this better than McCain himself, who has managed to charm reporters to such a degree that he forged an alliance that has become his greatest political asset.

When those reporters look at most politicians, they see both successes and failures, strengths and weaknesses, admirable traits and unsettling foibles. But over John McCain's career, critical events and features of his personality have been either overlooked or pushed to the background. This is not to say, however, that one cannot find mention of them if one looks hard enough. Whenever most of the news media miss a story or get it wrong, it is almost always the case that some reporter somewhere got it right. So when we say that something about McCain was ignored, or conversely that the media accepted a particular story line or interpretation, we don't mean that there was complete unanimity across every media outlet in the country. But the main contours of McCain's coverage have been so widespread and consistent that there is no mistaking them.

When a story, an event, or an interpretation emerges, it can have a variety of fates. It may simply disappear, little noticed and not long remembered. It may get repeated here and there, taking on a supporting role in the evolving picture of a candidate or a campaign. Or it may be woven integrally into that picture, so that it is repeated again and again, in story after story, by reporter after reporter, to the point where it becomes something everyone knows and accepts. This is the process by which our impressions of public figures are constructed. As we shall see, the stories that reporters retell about John McCain—and those they choose not to repeat—have added up to the most positive image of any contemporary politician.

There has been something approaching consensus on a critical set of interpretations of who John McCain is, what he has done, and what he represents. In most cases this consensus is driven by what is sometimes called the "elite media," those reporters who sit at the top of the news food chain. Although different analysts might disagree about which individuals constitute the elite media, few would dispute that today's news media are organized in a loosely hierarchical fashion, with places in that hierarchy determined in part—but by no means completely—by the size of the audience each journalist, commentator, or outlet commands.

At the top are the reporters, editors, and pundits who represent a small group of national news organizations: a few newspapers (particularly the *New York Times*, the *Washington Post*, *USA Today*, the *Wall Street Journal*, and the *Los Angeles Times*); the Associated Press news service; the three broadcast networks and the three cable networks; *Time* and *Newsweek* (and to a lesser extent, *U.S. News & World Report*); and National Public Radio. What distinguishes this small group, and what extends its influence beyond those who actually read or hear its words, is its ability to set the agenda for the rest of the news media. Even within the elite media there is an agenda-setting hierarchy: if Tim Russert of NBC's *Meet the Press* or the editors of the *New York Times* decide that a particular event is a big story, then the rest of the media will treat it as such. If they decide that a particular politician is an important figure whose views need to be heard, then other journalists will follow that cue as well.

When it comes to reporting on national politics, smaller news organizations often simply pass on news from these elite media. A small local paper doesn't have the resources to support a Washington bureau, so it runs stories provided by the Associated Press or the *New York Times* news service. If John McCain comes to town, the local television station will have neither the time nor the inclination to do extensive fresh reporting on McCain; it is far more likely to report the event and repeat what other news organizations have said about the Arizona senator.

But there is one group of local journalists whose reporting on John McCain is complex, nuanced, and far different from what one is likely to see in both the forty-nine other states and the national media. The reporters from Arizona—the ones who have known McCain the longest, seen him in the most varied situations, and come to understand him in the most complete way— paint a far different picture than that seen by citizens of the other forty-nine states. The mutual affection that characterizes his relationship with Washington-based reporters could hardly be more different than the testy relationship McCain has developed with journalists from his home state. That difference—how and why it developed—is a critical part of the story of McCain and the press.

The higher one proceeds up the media ladder, toward the most influential national print reporters and television personalities, the greater the admiration for John McCain seems to be. Before we begin our exploration of how that admiration arose and how it is manifested, we must stress that this book is not an investigation of John McCain, but a study of how the media have covered McCain. Those hoping to find previously unreported skeletons in the senator's closet will have to look elsewhere; all the information in this book comes from publicly available sources. What is the full picture of John McCain? How does it compare to the glowing picture painted by the media, and what is it that the public is missing in the coverage? What are the recurring themes and tropes in press coverage that have come to define John McCain? Why has the press given him such positive coverage? Despite his ideological distance from the moderate mainstream (not to mention from many of the reporters who display such affection for him), why do journalists continue to paint him as a symbol of apolitical moderation? How has he succeeded in winning their affections when so many other politicians have tried and failed?

John McCain very nearly won the Republican presidential nomination in 2000, and may do so in 2008. But in contrast to the scrutiny that the media have given previous would-be presidents—scrutiny that has ended its fair share of campaigns—the press has given McCain a free ride. In a media-centric political climate, the public relies on the press to cover its leaders with rigor, diligence, and skepticism. John McCain should be no exception.

Free Ride

Chapter 1

How He Won Their Hearts

Steve: *My friend and I have this argument, and here it is. He says when you're at a place like this, you can't just be yourself, you need an act. So anyway, I saw you standing there, so I thought, A, I could just leave you alone; B, I could come up with an act; or C, I could just be myself. I chose C. What do you think?*

Linda: *I think that A, you have an act, and that B, not having an act is your act.*

—*Singles* (1992)

There's no doubt about it: John McCain is a popular guy. In an age of partisan rancor, he gets favorable ratings not just from members of his own party, but from plenty of independents and Democrats as well. He is considered both ideologically moderate and someone to whom the excesses of contemporary politics—artificiality, nastiness, preferential treatment for financial backers—don't seem to apply.

But nowhere is McCain more popular than with the Washington, DC, journalistic establishment. Indeed, one struggles to recall a prominent political figure in recent decades who has received such sustained adulation from the ordinarily cynical press corps.

How did he do it? How did John McCain manage to turn a

pack of snarling beasts into obedient service animals, ready to do his bidding at every turn? As a starting point, it is important to keep in mind that it is, in fact, something McCain *did*, not something that happened by accident. While every politician seeks the best news coverage he or she can get, McCain employed a strategy that has been uniquely effective. And it is a strategy.

The Three Foundations

The press's affection for John McCain is built on three foundations: his Vietnam experience, his advocacy for campaign finance reform, and his style in dealing with reporters. McCain and his advisers display a deep understanding of how each functions, how to sustain their effectiveness, and how far they can be pushed. At first glance, these may seem like three very different matters: a factor of personal biography, a prosaic and often arcane policy issue, and a simple matter of personal relationships. But when it comes to McCain they actually have a great deal in common and add up to a portrait the press paints of the Arizona senator as not simply unlike other politicians, but the very antithesis of other politicians. Like a concave mirror, the prism through which the press views their subjects takes all that they dislike about politicians and inverts it to construct the figure of John McCain.

In all three cases, McCain has become for the press the opposite of everything they think is wrong with things as they are, and so he comes to embody for them the hope of a better politics. They view politicians as craven; McCain's undeniable courage in Vietnam casts him as the bravest of politicians, whether such bravery is truly in evidence at a particular moment or not. They view politicians as shameless supplicants to their contributors; McCain's advocacy of campaign finance reform makes him in their eyes the premier "reformer" in American politics (despite the weaknesses of the legislation he advocates and his spotty record on reform). They view politicians as cynically manipulative, fundamentally artificial, and endlessly hostile when it comes to dealing with journalists; McCain's attentive courting makes him "genuine" and "authentic" in a way no other politician can seem to achieve.

It is this last factor—the manner in which McCain has flattered, befriended, and courted reporters—that makes the other two factors meaningful. After all, there are other politicians who have heroic deeds in their past and have made efforts on behalf of reform. Like McCain, Ross Perot's 1992 running mate, James Stockdale, endured years in the Hanoi Hilton, but his Vietnam suffering didn't turn him into a press hero during his brief moment on the national stage; Republican congressman Sam Johnson of Texas was a prisoner of war in Vietnam for nearly seven years, but has never attracted any particular attention from the news media. Like McCain, Democrat Russell Feingold has spent much of his time in the Senate advocating political reform—indeed, Feingold's record on this front is superior to McCain's—but he is nowhere near the press favorite McCain is. In short, it is the combination of all three factors that produces McCain's unique status with the Washington press corps.

The result is that when McCain runs for office, he is described as the "anti-candidate"[1] (*Christian Science Monitor*) or "anti-politician" who runs an "anti-campaign"[2] (*New York Times*) and "refuse[s] to be scripted"[3] (*St. Petersburg Times*). The press uses McCain to define what it does not like about politicians and campaigns, a living rebuke to the shortcomings of modern politics.

Foundation 1: Vietnam

John McCain endured terrible suffering during the five and a half years he spent as a prisoner of war in Vietnam, and in the course of that time he displayed admirable courage, even heroism. No one would contest those facts. But it does not necessarily follow that McCain's Vietnam history should function as a halo reducing all questions of character—a press obsession, particularly when it comes to presidential candidates—to the story of the Hanoi Hilton. To be sure, McCain's Vietnam experience is a key part of his character, but it is, after all, only a part.

But that is not how the press sees it. It does not minimize McCain's courage and suffering in Vietnam to note that for no other politician does something that happened nearly forty years prior play such a prominent role in their own candidacy and in how the press discusses that candidacy. Other candidates—John F. Kennedy, George H. W. Bush, Bob Dole, and John Kerry, to name a few—have used their war records as selling points. Indeed, American politicians ever since George Washington have found political benefit in their military history. But war service was a *part* of the story those politicians told about themselves and the story the press told the public about them. For McCain, on the other hand, Vietnam is nearly the entirety of the character story we are told.

Other politicians find features of their biographies mentioned when they are relevant to the story at hand. The fact that John Kerry is a Vietnam veteran might be brought up by a journalist doing a story about, say, a proposal Kerry made on veterans' benefits. Dick Cheney's tenure as CEO of Halliburton will be discussed in a story about the White House and military contracting.

But McCain's POW experience is different. Journalists do not hesitate to mention it even when it has absolutely nothing to do with the story; instead, it is often tossed into stories by reporters almost in an offhand way, as though it were necessary to constantly remind readers of his trials. To take a typical example, a May 2006 *Christian Science Monitor* piece previewing the 2008 presidential race contained this sentence: "But conversation inevitably turns to Arizona's Sen. John McCain, whose directness sometimes disturbs his conservative colleagues, but whose valor while a prisoner of war in Vietnam enamors many voters."[4] There have been literally hundreds of articles that include a line on the order of "McCain, who spent five and a half years as a prisoner of war . . . ," as though that were his middle name. And not just when it comes to topics like the treatment of prisoners in Iraq or Vietnam itself. Often it is offered as a simple description of who McCain is. When McCain endorsed Charlie Crist for the Florida governorship, the *St. Petersburg Times* wrote, "McCain called Crist a reformer who's right on the issues. McCain is a decorated Vietnam War veteran and former prisoner of war and a likely 2008 Republican presidential candidate."[5] When he comes to town, local papers will make sure to remind readers who he is: "McCain, a Navy officer and former prisoner of war in Vietnam, is in his fourth term as senator from Arizona and ran for the Republican nomination for president in 2000. He's planning to return to Alabama in October to headline the Jefferson and Shelby counties' 'Grand Ol' Dinner,'" read an article in the *Birmingham News*.[6] At other times, his POW experience will be mentioned as a narrative technique to contextualize something else—like his reputation as a maverick. "John McCain, as a Navy pilot shot down over Hanoi, took a five-year beating from his Vietnamese jailers for refusing to break," wrote the *Washington Times*. "Sen. John McCain, 61, is

being battered now by fellow Republicans, this time for ideological deviations usually associated with exponents of big government, and only with words."[7]

One finds the line popping up as a non sequitur in articles
about budget disputes ("Arizona Sen. McCain, who spent five
years in a North Vietnamese prison, criticized fellow Republicans
on Tuesday for pushing for more tax cuts while U.S. troops were
fighting in Iraq and Afghanistan"—Associated Press),[8] legislation
on Internet gambling ("But with the war now apparently winding
down, McCain said he will reintroduce a sports betting ban bill
'soon,' although he declined to give a date. 'I was waiting until the
war kind of quieted down,' said McCain, who spent 5½ years as a
prisoner of war in Vietnam"—*Las Vegas Review-Journal*),[9] the role
of faith in politics ("The questioner noted President George
Bush's frequent reference to his Christian faith. No great leader
ever served without relying on faith, said McCain, a five-year prisoner of war in Vietnam"—Baton Rouge *Advocate*),[10] or even his
bout with skin cancer ("McCain, who spent 5½ years as a prisoner
of war in North Vietnam, was expected to make a statement later
Friday after meeting with his physicians at the Mayo Clinic in
nearby Scottsdale, Ariz."—*Chicago Tribune*).[11] One *Newsweek* story
from the 2000 campaign related how McCain responded when
someone insulted his wife: "McCain remained impassive. He was
trying to maintain what sailors call 'a steady strain,' a nautical term
for keeping the right amount of tension on a rope. It was
McCain's own defense mechanism, developed during five and a
half years of captivity, a private caution against letting your hopes
get too high or too low."[12] Either the reporter just assumed that
McCain's reaction had something to do with his POW experience,
or McCain later told him that was what he was doing. Either way,
it got a reminder of Vietnam into the story.

McCain's POW history even turns up in pop culture: an October 2006 episode of the CBS reality show *The Amazing Race* sent contestants to the Hanoi Hilton, where they had to find McCain's flight suit to locate the clue that would guide them to their next destination (McCain himself has also appeared on the screen, including cameos in the film *Wedding Crashers* and the television series *24*, and hosting *Saturday Night Live*). On the news, events with only the most tenuous connection to McCain can become an excuse for reminding the public that McCain was a prisoner of war. One May 2006 story on ABC's *World News* about the Navy sinking the aircraft carrier *Oriskany* to form a reef started as a nostalgic story about an old ship, but then turned into a virtual campaign ad for John McCain, complete with photos of him from Vietnam ("McCain remembers his final takeoff from the carrier in 1967, the day he was shot down, the start of five years of captivity").[13]

In fact, seldom does a day go by when somewhere in the American media some reporter is not reminding us that, in case you weren't aware of it, John McCain was a POW in Vietnam. As the figure below shows, at times the cascade of stories with references to McCain's captivity has been positively torrential.[14] The number of such mentions was highest in 1999 and 2000 during his first presidential campaign, subsided somewhat from 2001 to 2003, then picked up again in 2004.

A key part of McCain's Vietnam story as the press tells it is that the senator is reluctant to mention it. "One of the things I've never tried to do is exploit my Vietnam service to my country because it would be totally inappropriate to do so," McCain once said.[15] But for someone who says he doesn't want to talk about his experience as a POW, McCain sure does bring it up a lot. Consider a long 1999 article in *Esquire*, titled, with no apparent

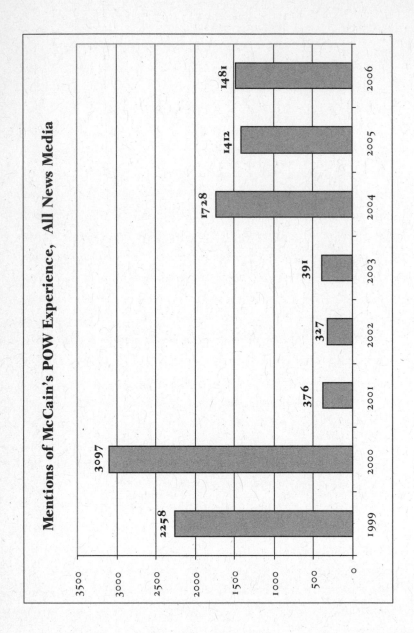

Mentions of McCain's POW Experience, All News Media

sarcasm, "John McCain Walks on Water." McCain told the reporter, "When somebody introduces me like, 'Here is our great war hero,' I don't like it. I want to be known as the guy who's trying to reform the telecommunications business, who's trying to see the cable rates deregulated. I mean, Jesus, it can make your skin crawl."[16] Yet from the very beginning of his political career, McCain has known just when to pull out his POW history for maximum effect. The key moment of his first congressional race came in a debate when McCain responded to an accusation of carpetbagging by saying, "As a matter of fact, when I think about it now, the place I lived longest in my life was Hanoi." Questioned about whether he was supporting George W. Bush's reelection with enough enthusiasm, McCain said, "There's this continued buzz out there that I do some of the things I do because I'm angry about the 2000 campaign. My response to that is that I forgave the Vietnamese and have worked for thirty years to heal the wounds of the Vietnam War. If I can get over that, am I going to hold a grudge because of a political campaign? I don't think so."[17] Asked why he was running for president, McCain joked, "Well, my wife, Cindy, believes it's because I received several sharp blows to the head while I was in prison."[18]

McCain's insistence that he doesn't want to talk about Vietnam is further belied by the fact that he built his entire 2000 campaign for the presidency around the POW story. His first television advertisement in New Hampshire was a sixty-second spot featuring black-and-white still photographs and footage of McCain as a young fighter pilot. Another ad featured McCain strolling through Arlington National Cemetery (later, the ad had to be edited to comply with Army regulations that prohibit partisan activity on cemetery grounds).[19] *Faith of My Fathers*, McCain's memoir of his wartime experience, came out in 1999, conveniently timed for the start of his campaign. Unlike the typical campaign book, it did not survey McCain's entire life, just his time in Vietnam. The dominant image of McCain displayed throughout his run was of him in a Navy flight suit, standing next to a jet, in 1965. Poster-sized copies were available for $15 on his campaign Web site.

Nor has his 2008 campaign hesitated to use McCain's Vietnam story. In March 2007, they sent out an e-mail marking the anniversary of McCain's release from the Hanoi Hilton, retelling the story of his captivity. A week later, another e-mail went out, this one including a note from a young girl, who wrote, "Dear Senator McCain: I love you. You are special. Thank you for sacrificing yourself for the freedom of our country. This is part of a song that describes you: I am free today for many gave their lives (like you). Love, Anna." Yet the question of whether McCain was inappropriately exploiting his suffering was never raised. Contrast that with what happened when John and Elizabeth Edwards announced in March 2007 that the candidate's wife had experienced a recurrence of breast cancer. Though the news coverage was unanimously sympathetic, the question of whether Edwards would be seen to be exploiting that sympathy was raised almost immediately in news stories and on television chat shows.

In fact, when one looks over McCain's career, one sees that at nearly every key moment, he has reaped political benefit from bringing up Vietnam. His first race for Congress was built on his Vietnam heroism. In his keynote speech at the 1996 Republican convention, which brought him into the national spotlight, he told the crowd how when he was in captivity in Hanoi, Republican nominee Bob Dole had worn a POW bracelet with McCain's name on it.

These are just a few examples that illustrate that McCain is perfectly willing to use his POW experience to make a point, whether serious or humorous. Indeed, that experience has always been McCain's political ace in the hole, the card he plays when he is in trouble or when the political moment calls for a knockout blow. "Even the Vietnamese didn't question my ethics," McCain told reporters quizzing him on his dealings with disgraced Savings and Loan scandal figure Charles Keating.[20] More recently, McCain ended an interview with Tim Russert on *Meet the Press* with a passive-aggressive sally: "I haven't had so much fun since my last interrogation."[21] If it sounded familiar, it was because McCain has made the same joke many times before. About watching the Arizona Diamondbacks lose a game to the Yankees in the 2001 World Series, he said, "I hadn't had so much fun since my last interrogation in Hanoi."[22] About campaigning in New Hampshire, he told Larry King in 1999, "Some of these places I haven't had so much fun since my last interrogation."[23] When in 1998 he lost a vote on a tobacco control bill and the Supreme Court struck down the line-item veto he had pushed, he said, "It's been a wonderful two weeks for me. I haven't had quite this much fun since I was interrogated in Hanoi."[24] Asked what it was like to be scrutinized as a potential vice presidential candidate in 1996, he said, "I haven't had so much fun since my last interrogation."[25]

McCain's speeches are judiciously peppered with anecdotes about the war, if not always about him. Instead of embracing his hero status, he often says that he served with heroes. "It doesn't take a lot of talent to get shot down," he has said. Taken on their own, such statements may seem charming in their modesty. But seen in the context of a permanent campaign that has transformed him into a political icon courtesy of his battle scars, it's hard not to view the self-effacing talk about his Vietnam experience as (as one Arizona reporter put it) "strategy disguised as humility."[26] What McCain no doubt understands is that *any* mention of Vietnam, even in the context of praising the service of others, will be enough to ensure that the story that results will include a reminder of McCain's POW experience.

Of course, McCain has every right to bring up Vietnam as often as he wishes. It is his history, and no one has ever suggested that he embellished or exaggerated it in any way. But what is striking is that reporters continue to insist on McCain's reticence when it comes to the topic, echoing the same dishonest assertion McCain makes. "Unlike Sen. John Kerry," wrote Bill Sammon of the *Washington Examiner*, "McCain rarely mentions his Vietnam service without prompting."[27] Or as Howard Kurtz of the *Washington Post* once wrote, "McCain doesn't talk much about those days, but he doesn't have to."[28] The truth is that he does talk about it, but even if he didn't, reporters would be sure to do it for him.

Consider an extraordinary 8,800-word love letter in the August 2006 issue of *Esquire*, in which reporter Chris Jones relates how McCain tells a joke at a fund-raiser comparing being vice president to his time in the Hanoi Hilton—evidence, one might suppose, that McCain is quite willing to mention his Vietnam experience. But Jones then writes this:

> McCain keeps his own collection of medals—a Silver Star, a Bronze Star, the Legion of Merit, a Distinguished Flying Cross, and his own Purple Heart—under wraps, although he is reminded of his exploits as a naval aviator at most of his public appearances, usually during the glowing introductions given by his hosts . . . Even now, nearly forty years later, he is reluctant to talk about it, except to say, "I have never considered myself a hero, because I failed in some ways." For him, Vietnam is not

the stuff of political capital. Rather, it is the reason why he cannot raise his arms high enough to comb his own hair.[29]

Note again: the *Esquire* reporter writes poetically about how
reluctant McCain is to mention Vietnam, *just after reporting how
McCain brought up Vietnam at a fund-raiser.* This piece brought to
mind a parody written by David Plotz in 1998 of the way reporters
would offer McCain's prisoner of war experience as all their readers needed to know about McCain:

> It is this arm, this right arm, that North Vietnamese torturers
> worked over for days in a hellhole called the Plantation, till it
> was broken and bruised and lacerated. It is this arm, this right
> arm, that is still stiff, still scarred, still bent. And it is this arm,
> this right arm, that the avaricious barons of tobacco, who sell
> death and call it commerce, think they can twist, think they can
> break, think they can make reach out to them, open-palmed.
>
> But, you see, they don't understand that this arm has a man
> attached to it. And they don't understand that the man is Sen.
> John McCain, who is allergic to their blandishments and
> threats, just as he is allergic to the cozy, sleazy compromises of
> this dark city, just as he is allergic to the mendacious hypocrisies
> of politics as it is practiced in late-20th-century America. For
> Sen. John McCain is the last _____ (man of honor, hero, hon-
> est man, saint . . .) in American politics. And perhaps, if we are
> very lucky, he is our next president . . .[30]

At times, the reminders come not just from McCain himself,
but from those close to him as well. When in 2000 someone asked
McCain's younger brother Joe, who was campaigning for him,
whether there was a problem with the fact that McCain was

accepting contributions from corporate lobbyists while advocating reform, Joe said, "This man had a chance to get out of POW
camp seven times; he stayed for five and a half years because it
was his duty. The Vietnamese tried to break him with clubs, iron
bars, torture, beating, isolation; they tried to break down his character, his integrity. If he can withstand that, is he gonna be
tempted by some guy in a blue suit with a fat wallet?"[31] In May
2006, McCain gave the commencement address at the New
School in New York. The class speaker, Jean Rohe, gave a speech
criticizing McCain's position on the Iraq war and then soon after
wrote about her speech on the *Huffington Post*. Mark Salter,
McCain's longtime aide and coauthor, offered a vigorous response
in the comments section, including this passage:

> Let me tell you a little bit about the Senator, the man you
> dismiss so derisively. Once upon a time, even among the young,
> the words courage and hero were used more sparingly, more
> precisely. It took no courage to do what you did, Ms. Rohe. It
> was an act of vanity and nothing more. And please don't worry
> about the Senator's discomfort with you. He has managed to
> endure much worse. McCain was once offered release from
> imprisonment and torture because of his father's position as a
> senior military officer. He declined because he would not leave
> his comrades behind, and thus, willingly, accepted four more
> years of hardships life will spare almost all of us from. In his
> political career he has shown the same character he showed as a
> Navy officer all those years ago. He has, over and over again,
> risked personal ambitions for what he believes, rightly or
> wrongly, are in the best interests of the country. What, pray tell,
> have you risked?[32]

Anyone miss the message? Rohe was wrong to criticize McCain, because McCain was a prisoner of war decades before. Thus his Vietnam experience can be not just a political tool but a cudgel with which to bludgeon a college student who criticized his position on Iraq. It should be noted that other than McCain himself, there is no one more responsible for the creation and maintenance of the Myth of McCain than Salter, who has worked for the senator for nearly two decades and coauthored the McCain books *Faith of My Fathers, Worth the Fighting For, Why Courage Matters,* and *Character Is Destiny.*

In short, McCain and his advisers have located a kind of sweet spot where they bring up his Vietnam history often enough to keep it in the forefront of discussions about him, but not so much that reporters conclude that he is trying to exploit it for political gain. Even when they fail to remind voters that he was once a prisoner of war, they can be sure reporters will again and again. And when they do, they will be sure to note McCain's reluctance.

The media's obeisance to McCain the war hero is manifest not just in what they say, but in what they don't say. Consider the case of Ted Sampley. In 2004, another Vietnam veteran, John Kerry, made a run for the White House. During his campaign, Kerry was attacked by the right on his war service. One of the activists spearheading the attacks was Sampley, a former Green Beret and self-appointed POW/MIA advocate. Sampley and his group, Vietnam Veterans Against John Kerry, issued scurrilous charges against Kerry's war service, questioning his injuries, his awards, and his loyalty (Sampley's group was separate from the Swift Boat Veterans for Truth). Their allegations had the desired effect. Although many pundits criticized his irresponsible attacks, Sampley's accusations nevertheless appeared on the national radar screen. Newspapers and TV news shows devoted precious space and time to dignifying Sampley's outlandish remarks simply by repeating them. As the Rove war room would say, "Mission accomplished."

But Kerry has never been Sampley's only nemesis. In fact, John McCain has been in Sampley's crosshairs longer. In 1992, Sampley wrote a long article claiming that McCain was a "Manchurian candidate," a POW who collaborated with the Vietnamese and was programmed by the Soviets to betray the United States. In 2000, Sampley, abetted by the Bush team, mounted a campaign to bring down McCain's candidacy.[33] But in contrast to the exposure that the media would give Sampley's rantings in 2004, the media barely gave his assault on McCain any attention. Between November 1999 and November 2000, only *four* mentions of Sampley's attacks on McCain appeared in U.S. television news shows, newspapers, and magazines. Compare that with the exposure Sampley received when he attacked Kerry. During the same yearlong span in 2003–2004, there were more than seventy mentions of Sampley's charges against Kerry, including in-depth discussions on cable news shows.

When Sampley attacked McCain—with the imprimatur of the Bush campaign, which allowed Sampley to speak at a rally in South Carolina as Bush stood behind him—the media decided that his charges were too insane to be dignified with coverage. When Sampley attacked Kerry, however, the media displayed considerably lower standards. Sampley was quoted in major news outlets such as the Associated Press, the *New York Times*, the *Boston Globe*, the *Los Angeles Times*, and the *Atlanta Journal-Constitution*, and interviewed on NPR, MSNBC, and Fox News. Though many of the reports were critical of Sampley, the very appearance of his tirades in the media had precisely the agenda-setting effect that

Kerry's opponents desired. One might argue that Kerry was his party's nominee and therefore received greater scrutiny than McCain did as one of many Republican contenders. But it isn't as though McCain's Vietnam service was a topic reporters never got around to discussing.

There are a number of other Vietnam veterans who have served in the Senate and even run for president, none of whom got the same treatment McCain does. So just what is it about McCain's experience that generates not only reverence but such continued attention from the press? It is more than the fact that McCain was tortured or that he displayed admirable courage at the time. Writing in the *New Republic* in 1999, David Grann offered an insightful analysis of the symbolic power of McCain's Vietnam experience:

In Vietnam, McCain did precisely what Clinton did not: he fought, and did so voluntarily. What's more, in a war in which, as Phil Caputo once wrote, Americans "had done nothing more than endure," McCain, who had endured more than anyone, reinvented the myth of the war hero, which had largely been shattered by the nightly footage of napalm bombings and body counts.

Unlike Eisenhower or Ulysses S. Grant, the traditional war icons, McCain did not take a hill or liberate a city; he did not sneak behind enemy lines or sink a ship. He went to prison and was tortured. In some sense, he became an emblem of the nation's suffering, a metaphor of all the people imprisoned by the war—"trapped in it, trapped by it, trapped against it," as Todd Gitlin, the '60s activist and author, put it to me. In a war of victims, McCain had become the ultimate one. The tragic hero.[34]

McCain thus becomes the perfect Vietnam candidate, the one whose service everyone can admire without reservation, no matter how you felt or feel about the war itself. He didn't avoid going, like Bill Clinton and George W. Bush. He didn't turn against the war and become an opponent, like Kerry. He doesn't present himself as a gung-ho supporter. He went, and he suffered. In 2004, as the Swift Boat Veterans for Truth were spreading their dossier of lies about Kerry and the wounds of the war seemed to be opening all over again, McCain made a very public plea to put the issue aside once and for all, something most Americans were probably feeling (though McCain later employed the same media consulting firm, Stevens Reed Curcio & Potholm, that produced the Swift Boat ads he denounced).

It casts no aspersions on McCain's Vietnam experience to observe that he has a highly nuanced understanding of how to use this history to his political advantage. Perhaps reporters believe that questioning the way he has done so would sound as though they were questioning McCain's moral stature as a former POW or denying the magnitude of what he endured. And since few of the reporters who cover him were themselves in the armed forces in Vietnam, there may be no small measure of guilt involved, or at least the belief that they have not earned the right to ask him critical questions. On a 2006 episode of *Hardball*, Bloomberg News reporter Roger Simon noted that reporters have given McCain "a break or two or three or four or five hundred," to which host Chris Matthews immediately replied, "Because he served in Vietnam, and a lot of us didn't."[35] "McCain, after all, spent five and half years in a prisoner of war camp," noted *Editor & Publisher*. "He courted the male, baby boomer journalists who had avoided the Vietnam conflict, protested it, or were too young to fight in it."[36] In response, they testify that his POW experience is not only the sum total of McCain's "character," but constitutes the lens through which character itself must be viewed in any race in which McCain participates. When Amy Silverman of the *Phoenix New Times* interviewed a series of reporters for a 1997 story about McCain's relationship to the press, she wrote of the POW experience, "Every journalist interviewed for this story mentions it right off the bat." "You can't deny the fact that he is a bona fide, walkin' talkin' John Wayne character," the *Washingtonian*'s Harry Jaffe told her. "That lays a foundation of respect."[37] There is little evidence that much has changed in the decade since.

Foundation 2: Campaign Finance Reform

Campaign finance reform may seem like a prosaic issue, surely not a wellspring of the grand poetry out of which successful national campaigns are built. Yet it served as the defining policy issue of not only McCain's 2000 race but his entire career, and it is one of the pillars on which his relationship with the press was built.

The McCain-Feingold bill (ultimately termed the Bipartisan Campaign Reform Act of 2002) was introduced in 1997, along with companion legislation in the House of Representatives. The main feature of the bill was a ban on "soft money"—the unlimited donations to political parties that had been legal up until the bill's passage. The fact that individuals and corporations could skirt contribution limits by giving large donations to the parties (sometimes in amounts running into the millions) had been a complaint of critics for some time. The ensuing five years would see fits and starts, ups and downs, and the eventual passage of the bill into law with President Bush's signature in 2002. During that time an extraordinary amount of media coverage was given to the bill and the cause of campaign finance reform more broadly, most of it positive.

Conservative media critics may not be right about much, but when they charged that the news media tended to portray campaign finance reform in a favorable light, they were probably right. It was certainly the case that most prominent newspaper editorial pages favored the passage of McCain-Feingold, and said so in editorial after editorial. The loudest cheerleaders were the editorial pages of the *Washington Post* and the *New York Times*; between them the two papers wrote more than three hundred editorials between 1997 and 2002 in favor of either campaign finance reform in general or McCain-Feingold in particular.[38]

Every epic tale needs a hero, and so McCain was the hero of the campaign finance reform narrative. The story the press told was about a lonely man fighting overwhelming odds, waging a noble campaign to clean up the system, with only perseverance and justice on his side. "There is a Don Quixote aspect to the so-called McCain-Feingold reform bill in that it seems at times as if the two men are tilting at windmills," wrote the *Chicago Tribune*.[39] "He's been fighting a lonely battle for campaign finance reform against the wishes of the party leadership," said CBS News.[40] But in truth, he wasn't all that lonely—at the time virtually all the Democrats in Congress supported McCain-Feingold, as did the president and the majority of the public. And when the bill was first introduced, it was often referred to in the press as "Feingold-McCain." But McCain soon took center stage; that appellation disappeared and McCain's name always appeared first.[41] As on many other subjects, McCain was portrayed as taking a risky stand, when in fact his position was overwhelmingly popular with the public. Despite the fact that the issue ranked low on the list of voters' priorities, surveys consistently showed strong support for the bill's centerpiece, the banning of soft money donations. As much as two-thirds of the public favored such a ban.[42]

But why was campaign finance reform such a powerful issue for McCain when it came to the press? After all, there are many issues on which editorial boards agree, and their advocates do not garner the kind of journalistic worship that McCain received. The answer is that the issue of campaign finance reform, and the McCain-Feingold bill in particular, became a vessel into which the press could pour all of its disgust with the practice of politics. The details of the bill, and whether it would truly be effective in curbing the influence of special interests, ended up being almost beside the point. The issue gave the press the opportunity to write about all the terrible things it sees on Capitol Hill: the blatant buying of influence, the shameful groveling for campaign contributions, the symbiotic relationship between those who hold power and those who want the powerful to bestow gifts upon them.

As campaign finance reform's champion, McCain became a symbol of what could be right in politics, the "independent" free of influence by moneyed elites, the "reformer" out to clean up the system, a man motivated by conviction and nothing else, as pure as the driven snow. When McCain-Feingold and its companion bill in the House, Shays-Meehan (sponsored by Republican Christopher Shays and Democrat Martin Meehan) finally passed both houses of Congress in early 2002, the *New York Times* declared it "a victory for all Americans" in an editorial titled "An Extraordinary Victory."[43] Sounding a similar note, a *Washington Post* editorial read, "Breaking that link to big money may help reduce public cynicism about politics and elected officials. And that, as Sen. McCain said in his closing remarks, is a service to the country."[44]

Five years later, it would be difficult for anyone to argue that McCain-Feingold actually cleaned up the campaign finance system. It is true that by banning soft money, the legislation inserted a middleman between contributors and the parties. But many who used to write large checks to the parties now do the same to independent 527s (independent groups established for the purpose of influencing elections; the name comes from the section of the tax code that allows their existence). Rather than diminishing, the amount of money spent on political campaigns has exploded, and while there had previously been at least some accountability for the parties that received soft money and what they did with it, groups like the Swift Boat Veterans for Truth can poison a campaign with lies and distortions, and the mud won't rub off on the candidates on whose behalf they labor. Many have argued that a more comprehensive reform—a move to complete public financing of congressional elections, for instance—would accomplish far more in reducing both actual corruption and the appearance of corruption than McCain-Feingold ever could. (Though he did support Arizona's "Clean Money" law, which established public financing of state elections in 2002, McCain has never pushed for public financing of federal campaigns.)

There was one more element to McCain-Feingold that might have made McCain's involvement seem less noble: it had the effect of boosting the Republican Party at the expense of the Democratic Party. At the time, the Democrats relied much more heavily on soft money donations, particularly from labor unions, than did Republicans. The Republican Party, on the other hand, had a larger base of wealthy individuals who gave substantial contributions and so was not as affected when six-figure donations were banned. When the bill passed the House, the conservative editorial page of the *Wall Street Journal* assured its compatriots,

"Republicans shouldn't be alarmed, despite House Speaker Dennis Hastert's claim that Shays-Meehan could produce Armageddon for them. In truth, there's a better chance the measure will aid Republicans in winning the White House, Senate, and House, rather than impede them."[45] The *Atlantic Monthly* later reported that, in private, Republican election lawyers referred to McCain-Feingold as "the Democratic Party suicide bill."[46]

And McCain knew as well as anyone that his signature legislation would have the effect of boosting the Republican Party's fortunes. When Americans for Tax Reform aired an ad in New Hampshire in 1999 accusing him of helping Democrats by working to ban soft money, McCain's spokesman protested to the Associated Press, "In fact banning soft money will help the Republican Party because it will stop the flow of cash which runs around the clock from the big labor unions straight into the Democratic Party's coffers."[47]

Republicans offered a variety of reasons to explain their opposition to legislation that would help their party, but most centered on the libertarian grounds that people should be able to give parties as much money as they want without limits imposed by the government. Those who wanted more money in politics, not less, got a key change to the bill late in the process that unambiguously aided the GOP. With McCain's support, the bill raised, from $1,000 to $2,000, the maximum amount that individuals could donate to candidates, so-called hard money (the limit was also pegged to inflation so it would continue to increase). "That is a godsend to President Bush," said Larry Sabato of the University of Virginia, noting the GOP's greater strength among wealthy individuals, who could now give their favored candidates twice as much money as they had in the past.[48]

In order to understand why the press viewed campaign finance reform so positively, one must appreciate that coverage of Congress is overwhelmingly negative—stories about gridlock, shady backroom deals, bitter partisanship, and unjustifiable pork far outnumber stories about noble legislators and reasonable compromises. The surest way for a member of Congress to get on the evening news is to make a vicious attack on someone from the other party. The result is that the Congress shown on the news is a moral cesspool populated by venal politicians who would sell out their own mothers for a few extra campaign contributions. Although we cannot say with certainty what lies within the hearts of the Capitol Hill press corps, it would be strange if this coverage did not reflect, at least to some extent, their general outlook on the institution they cover. The old aphorism states that laws and sausages are the two things one should never watch being made; as those who spend their days wandering the halls of the sausage factory, Capitol Hill reporters almost inevitably grow cynical, even disgusted, about the legislative process.

What occurred during the long debate on McCain-Feingold was a startling outbreak of hope among the press, hope that national politics could be rid of some of its more unsavory features. The villain in this story was the system itself, a voracious beast devouring any principled person who stepped in the muck-filled halls of Congress. There was no doubt who the hero was, and it wasn't Russell Feingold, Christopher Shays, or Martin Meehan. It was John McCain, and the battle forever ensured that when reporters think "reformer," the first name that pops into their heads is McCain's.

Recall the argument McCain's chief of staff Mark Salter made: "In his political career he has shown the same character he showed as a Navy officer all those years ago. He has, over and over again, risked personal ambitions for what he believes, rightly or wrongly, are in the best interests of the country." Salter was no doubt referring in part to McCain's great crusade of campaign finance reform. But as in most of the cases in which McCain contradicts the majority of his party, he was in truth taking no risk at all. While most Republicans took the opposite position on the issue, McCain never displayed any interest in rising to a leadership position in the Senate, the only ambition that would have been immediately compromised by his advocacy for campaign finance reform. Instead, his sights were set higher, and the issue was nothing but a benefit in that effort: he took a popular position, one that almost guaranteed him positive press coverage. There was virtually no risk of public displeasure; one poll taken after the bill passed found only 14 percent of Americans favoring a presidential veto of McCain-Feingold.[49] And his campaign had the side benefit of helping the Republican Party and hurting the Democrats. No one should believe for a moment that opposing most Republicans on campaign finance reform constituted any risk to John McCain's personal ambitions. Whatever the merits of McCain's position on the issue, taking it was no great act of courage.

In sum, McCain's great triumph of maverick rebellion and bipartisanship: 1) damaged the Democratic Party by eliminating the one fund-raising area, soft money, in which they had an advantage over Republicans; 2) allowed wealthy donors, most of whom are Republican, to give more money to Republican candidates; and 3) allowed the total amount of special interest money pouring into political campaigns to increase, not decrease.

Yet these facts have done nothing to diminish John McCain's place as the avatar of political reform. Whenever a reform of any sort is proposed, reporters rush to find out what John McCain thinks, and news stories about government waste and pork are inevitably peppered with the obligatory condemnatory McCain quote or paraphrase, so generic as to make one wonder whether the reporter even bothered to speak to the senator. Wherever the press sees Congress as bad, John McCain is the one person who comes across as unsullied. If the institution is no cleaner for his presence, it must be only because the problems are so intractable that not even McCain can overcome them. But his reform "crusade" has hardly been for naught; it has solidified the idea that he above all others is a man of principle willing to fight tough battles in the service of what is right.

Foundation 3: I Love You, You Love Me

I never saw Heifetz play the violin, or Hogan hit a five iron, or Pavlova do a pirouette. But I've seen John McCain work a reporter.

And I knew I was seeing a master at the peak of his form.

Here's what happens. The reporter—call him Joe—hops aboard McCain's old campaign bus, the Straight Talk Express. He knows the Arizona senator's well-known charms. He will not be seduced.

Chatting amiably, Joe asks about a Republican colleague. With ironic solemnity, McCain responds by describing his fellow senator with an anatomical epithet. Against his better judgment, Joe chuckles. (Never heard that from a presidential candidate before!)

He asks a probing question about McCain's personal life—and the senator answers without hesitation, never asking to go off the record. (Is there nothing this guy won't be candid about?)

Joe's detachment is already crumbling when McCain offhandedly mentions a self-deprecating anecdote from his time "in prison." The reporter knows the reference is to McCain's years as a POW in Vietnam, back when Joe was sucking bong hits at Princeton. (Guilt, guilt, guilt . . .)

McCain asks Joe about his kids, by name, then recommends a new book he's been reading—something unexpectedly literary (I.B. Singer's short stories?). Seamlessly, he mentions an article Joe wrote—not last week, but in 1993!

The reporter has never voted for a Republican in his life. But he's a goner.[50]

—Andrew Ferguson, *Bloomberg News*

Candidates have always painted themselves as regular folks possessed of the heartland's simple virtues, from Abe Lincoln learning the value of hard work in his log cabin to George W. Bush clearing brush on his "ranch." But with television's gradual takeover of presidential politics, "authenticity" became a function not of background and biography but of style. The candidate who would garner the highest praise was not the wisest or the most experienced but the one who was "real," who could speak to regular people in their language and convince them he was "one of them." Commentator Mark Schmitt has called this the "cult of authenticity," the press's obsession with determining which candidate is more genuine and showering praise on those who pass the test—and withering contempt on those who fail. Eventually, the press began to act as though the most important qualification for holding the most powerful office in the world was whether people wanted to have a beer with you.

This transformation didn't happen the moment politics entered the modern age, however. The first televised campaign was in 1952, and a stiffer, more awkward candidate than Dwight Eisenhower, who won that race and the next, was seen neither before nor since. It was not until Ronald Reagan that a politician was able to utilize the televised medium to its full effect. What Reagan understood was that television turns a candidate from someone speaking far away on a podium to someone talking one-on-one with the voter. Television frames politicians at an intimate distance and allows for a quieter tone of voice. So Reagan used a more conversational style than had his predecessors, eschewing poetry and metaphor in favor of vernacular speech and storytelling.

At the same time, television elevated the importance of attributes like good looks and a pleasant voice that reasonable people, reporters included, might say should have little bearing on how we choose our leaders. So as a parade of politicians who could pass for local TV meteorologists ascended to public office, reporters became more and more turned off by those they came to believe were blow-dried, smooth-talking, and ultimately lacking in substance.

During the same period, reporters began to see their jobs as not just reporting on what the candidate did in public, but getting the story *behind* the story, the hidden strategies and revealing moments kept out of the public's view. When Theodore White published *The Making of the President 1960*, his behind-the-scenes story of that race, it forever changed campaign journalism. White told a dramatic tale in which John F. Kennedy was the hero, and journalists immediately began looking to emulate White's style by probing their subjects to uncover the "real" man behind the public image. Two subsequent books also had an enormous influence: *The Presidential Character*, in which political scientist James David Barber argued that what mattered in presidents was not their agendas but their psychology and character; and *The Selling of the President*, Joe McGinniss's take on Richard Nixon's 1968 campaign, in which he portrayed Nixon's handlers selling him to the public as though he were a new brand of laundry detergent. While White's book taught journalists how they should report a campaign, Barber and McGinniss taught them what perspective they should bring.

This is not to say, however, that getting positive press coverage became a simple matter for candidates. There are many routes to good coverage, many varieties of spin—and just as many ways for a candidate to fail. John Kerry, for instance, was chided for his ability to see "nuance"; just before the first general election debate of 2004, NBC's Andrea Mitchell said, "[Kerry] has not shown that he can crisply and definitively explain himself in sound bites. He's got to talk in sound bites . . . What Bush is very good at doing . . . is repeating over and over the same message."[51]

So it is not so much spin per se that reporters don't like, but unsuccessful spin, particularly if it looks strained (and of course, it is the reporters themselves who determine which spin is successful). By the same token, as consumed as they are with "authenticity," what they truly value is not authenticity but a convincing portrayal of the authentic. George W. Bush—son of a president, grandson of a senator, educated at Andover, Yale, and Harvard, who personally selects the fabric for his custom-made $3,000 suits[52]—is no more a "regular guy" than the two men he defeated to take and hold the White House, but he is a much better actor than either. His regular-guy act was lauded for its verisimilitude, while his opponents' acts were derided as phony. Carl Cameron of Fox News, one of Bush's biggest fans in the press corps, once said, "The problem for Kerry may be who he is. An Ivy League millionaire, who has rubbed elbows with the world's wealthiest sophisticates, while most of rural America is considered Bush country. Close your eyes and Kerry's praise for the heartland and its voters sounds a lot like something President Bush might say."[53] When Ivy League millionaire George Bush praises the heartland, on the other hand, it's *real.*

So it should be uncontroversial to assert that every politician, when he or she speaks to reporters or appears on television, is in some ways enacting a performance. No human being is completely him- or herself when speaking in front of cameras, and politicians are particularly attuned to how they are perceived by others. Some performances are more convincing than others, and some seem forced while others seem natural, but they are all performances.

But the cynical reporters who often portray politics as a combination of theater and con game seem to exclude the very possibility that they are witnessing a performance when the performer is John McCain. In fact, the senator from Arizona has managed to achieve a miraculous kind of anti-spin. Like the character in *Singles* we quoted at the beginning of this chapter, McCain has an act, and not having an act is his act. But unlike the savvy woman in the film who sees right through it, reporters have fallen for it hard.

Most politicians have an understandable wariness when it comes to dealing with reporters. After all, those reporters are just waiting for the politician to make a mistake, to say something controversial or embarrassing, to plant a foot firmly in his or her own mouth. So they grow careful, measured in their statements, hewing closely to a strategy designed to deliver a message while steering clear of anything interesting. Needless to say, reporters find this tendency endlessly frustrating. Eager to fill their copy with something other than talking points, they grow resentful of the more spin-prone politicians—particularly those who deliver the same talking points when they are in informal settings with reporters instead of loosening up—and thus more ready to bring the hammer down when the politicians finally do utter a gaffe. So the politician becomes even more careful, and the reporters hope more desperately for some crack in the armor to be revealed. (Part of George W. Bush's successful press relations was his willingness to hang out and joke with reporters when the cameras were turned off.)

John McCain found the way to break through this vicious cycle. Instead of approaching them with caution, he would give reporters exactly what they want. He would barely ever go off the record. He would return their calls promptly. He would just chat, and chat, and chat some more, sometimes for hours. He would treat them like buddies, not measuring his words when they were in the room. "Reporters are so used to being spun," McCain has said. "If you just talk to them, and tell them what you really think, they appreciate it."[54] As *Editor & Publisher* noted, "Washington reporters especially loved him because he was a quote machine who could be turned on at three in the morning."[55]

By talking to them in a way that seemed uncalculated, McCain fundamentally reoriented the relationship between journalist and politician, so that instead of being adversaries, each distrusting the other and each trying to get something out of the other, McCain and the reporter begin to feel like *partners* in getting the reporter's job done. At least that's the way it seems from the reporter's point of view.

And what happened? The strategy worked like a charm. The reporters came to simply like McCain more than they do other politicians. As David Nyhan of the *Boston Globe* wrote in 1997, "For a lot of people the Senate is 99 bozos and this guy."[56] And the reports they produced—and continue to produce—about McCain are simply different than those about his colleagues. They take his good intentions and integrity for granted, assume he means what he says, and portray him over and over as someone who is not like other politicians. Among the many benefits for McCain is that when he does say something problematic, reporters brush it off, to a degree they never would with other politicians. McCain's friendly relationship with the press functions as a protective cloak shielding him from potentially damaging stories.

As Tish Durkin argued in the *National Journal* in 2001, the admiration for McCain is in part a function of low expectations. Most politicians are so careful and measured around reporters that even a tiny bit of apparent spontaneity can go a long way. "McCain is capable of chatting off the cuff," Durkin wrote. "He will utter a syllable that perhaps he shouldn't. This is enough to make him a rogue, a sage, a guru. The fact that McCain gets so far on what would elsewhere be considered minimum courtesies and marks of individuality is not a statement on how engaging or craven—take your pick—McCain is. It is a statement of how studiously dry and cautious almost everybody else is."[57]

There is also the element of flattery at work. When he worked on his father's presidential campaigns, George W. Bush was known to respond to questions from reporters with "No comment, asshole," as Bill Minutaglio reported in his widely praised biography, *First Son*.[58] As president, Bush may have worked hard to be personally friendly with reporters, giving each of them nicknames, but his administration's approach to their profession suggests that his fundamental views on them have not changed. Bush's message to reporters since assuming the presidency has been not just that he believes they are biased against him, but that they are fundamentally unimportant. As his chief of staff Andrew Card told the *New Yorker*, the Bush White House believes that reporters "don't represent the public any more than other people do. In our democracy, the people who represent the public stood for election. I don't believe you have a check-and-balance function."[59]

By courting them so assiduously, McCain tells reporters that they are important. If George W. Bush is the captain of the football team who pays attention to the geeks who work on the school newspaper only when he decides to give them a punch in the arm, McCain is the popular kid who, despite his revered status, will sit down with those geeks in the cafeteria and hang with them. Not only will he shine his charismatic light their way, he'll tell them—to their unending delight—how he thinks the newspaper is the glue that holds the whole school together.

And the image McCain has fashioned—that of the independent, straight-talking maverick unafraid to ruffle feathers—is particularly appealing to reporters, who would like to see themselves in the same way. "Who does the press like?" said Paul Starobin of the *National Journal*. "They like this guy who is sort of a maverick who doesn't get along with a lot of his own colleagues. So, in a way, he embodies some attributes—like iconoclasm and irreverence—that journalists themselves pride themselves on."[60] The idea that McCain fights against "the establishment" makes him all the more appealing. As Dick Polman of the *Philadelphia Inquirer* wrote in 2007, reporters "fell hard for McCain in 2000, not just because he granted so much access, but because he sold himself as a rebel, an antiestablishment reformer with no patience for political orthodoxy."[61]

The fact that his carefully chosen breaks with his party have caused some Republicans to speak angrily of McCain only increases reporters' admiration. "To the extent most reporters are forced to think about policy ideas at all, they favor those who run against the grain of partisanship," wrote ABC News's Mark Halperin and the *Washington Post*'s John Harris in their book *The Way to Win*. "The best way for a Democratic politician to get good Washington press is to announce, Joe Lieberman–style, that the party is too much in the grip of the teachers unions and Hollywood. The best way for a Republican to get good Washington press is to announce that the party has got to move beyond its conservative social agenda and have the 'courage' to increase taxes."[62] The particulars of taxes or the teachers unions notwithstanding, Halperin and Harris's point—that high-profile challenges to those in your party only increase your esteem in reporters' eyes—applies to no one better than McCain.

The particulars of McCain's courting of the press are familiar to some, but it is worth noting just how revolutionary his press strategy has been. In early 1999, the McCain presidential campaign began referring to its occasional tours through New Hampshire and other presidential primary states as the "Straight Talk Express." The name was not originally intended to be permanent, but after it became apparent that the theme of "straight talk" was paying dividends, the campaign bus itself was renamed.[63] As Tucker Carlson described it, the Straight Talk Express had a jovial, locker-room atmosphere, complete with free-flowing booze and plenty of swearing on the candidate's part. "After a day or two of this sort of thing," Carlson wrote, "the average journalist inevitably concluded that John McCain was about the coolest guy who ever ran for president . . . I saw reporters call McCain 'John,' sometimes even to his face and in public. I heard others, usually at night in the hotel bar, slip into the habit of referring to the McCain campaign as 'we'—as in, 'I hope we kill Bush.' It was wrong, but it was hard to resist."[64]

One of the key techniques McCain uses is to tell reporters a self-deprecating story without prompting. Unlike other politicians, who tend to portray themselves in the best possible light in every situation, McCain seems willing to lay bare his less flattering attributes. Another interpretation is that he understands that the best way to avoid having reporters trumpet unflattering things about you is to tell them first, before they get the chance to find out somewhere else. Veteran campaign reporter Roger Simon described the scene on the campaign bus this way:

> On one recent five-day tour of New Hampshire, his 15th Granite State trip since he began running for president, he unexpectedly began the day by volunteering to reporters some of the terrible things he has said in the past. First there was the time he referred to the Leisure World senior citizens home as

"Seizure World," and then there was the time he said, "The nice thing about Alzheimer's is you get to hide your own Easter eggs," and then there was the egregious joke that went something like, "Why is Chelsea Clinton so ugly? Janet Reno is her father, and Hillary is her mother," and pretty soon a reporter just begged McCain to shut up and protect himself. But the guy can't help it. He was a Navy jet jockey, and while regulations required him to follow a careful checklist before each takeoff, McCain often dispensed with it. "Kick the tires and light the fires!" McCain says, recalling his motto back then. "To hell with the checklist. Anybody can be slow." Which is exactly the way he is running his campaign.[65]

What is so notable about this passage is that even in an article whose topic was how enamored reporters are of McCain, Simon didn't seem to entertain the possibility that McCain rattling off his most embarrassing statements might be something more than a charming recklessness. Instead, "the guy can't help it. He was a Navy jet jockey . . ." On the other hand, could it be that by bringing up his prior statements, he ensures that reporters will yawn if anyone tries to use them against him? *What, the Chelsea Clinton joke? McCain talks about that all the time; why should we write a story about it?* Mission accomplished.

A closely related technique McCain uses is the mea culpa, offered not in a grandiose way during a press conference but almost offhand when chatting with reporters. It usually plays out this way: McCain engages in a blatantly political move; if it works, then the fact that it was carefully calculated is not discussed. As far as we know, McCain has never said to reporters, "That cynical political strategy I employed worked out great!" But if it fails, on the other hand, he then tells reporters how stupidly political it was, and how he wishes he had never done it. They are left not with the feeling that he is like other politicians in that he makes blatantly political moves, but that he is unlike other politicians because he admits mistakes.

As columnist Joe Klein wrote in his book *Politics Lost,* "Every time a new big shot boarded the bus, armed with gotcha questions and anxious to challenge the candidate's vaunted candor, McCain would disarm him in the simplest possible way: he would admit that he had made a mistake or gotten something wrong, or didn't know the answer. He did this constantly, and it was always successful."[66] Yet on the very next page, Klein argues that this technique is not a calculated piece of press management, but something that springs from the very core of McCain's being. "McCain's honesty about his own weaknesses was an exceptionally powerful political tool, and it probably stemmed from the fact that running for president was not the defining moment of his life, nor the most difficult thing he had ever done. He had been a prisoner of war in North Vietnam . . ." For Klein, as for so many others, McCain's POW experience renders anything McCain does comprehensible only through the most noble interpretation possible.

The result is not only that McCain gets better press coverage generally than other politicians, but that he escapes scrutiny on some of the same issues that bedevil others. Gary Hart was driven from the 1988 presidential race over accusations of marital infidelity, and Bill Clinton was dogged by the same questions four years later. Even though those alleged affairs took place closer to the campaign going on at the time, it would seem relevant that McCain, by his own admission, ruined his first marriage because of his philandering. And yet that fact is almost never mentioned in stories about McCain. For Hart and Clinton, marital fidelity was supposed to provide a window into their "character"—how many times did we hear someone ask, "If he'll cheat on his wife, how do we know he won't cheat the country?" But for McCain, who cheated on the woman who waited patiently for him during his years of captivity—and who was disabled as a result of a car crash while he was gone—adultery is not part of the "character" story that is told, not something voters are told should be used to evaluate whether he is the right man to be president.

Of course, this isn't to encourage such tawdry news coverage, but merely to point out the different standards the press uses for ordinary candidates and for John McCain. One could make a convincing case that the press's enthusiasm for sifting through politicians' personal lives serves no legitimate purpose. But it would be hard to argue that an issue like marital infidelity ought to matter for some candidates but not for others.

And few reporters seem to have wondered just how important personal charm—the skill that perhaps above all others has earned McCain his status with the press—ought to be in a potential president. One could easily argue that skill at charming people in informal settings is no more important to leadership than, say, the ability to give a great speech. When novelist David Foster Wallace traveled with the McCain campaign in 2000, he noted the difference:

> In fairness to McCain, he's not an orator and doesn't pretend to be. His real métier is conversation, a back-and-forth . . . So, while the media marvel at his accessibility because they've been trained to equate it with vulnerability, they don't seem to realize they're playing totally to McCain's strength when they converse with him instead of listening to his speeches. In conversation he's smart and alive and human and seems actually to listen and respond directly to you instead of to some

demographic abstraction you might represent. It's his speeches
and 22.5s [the precisely timed remarks with which McCain
would open his town hall meetings] that are canned and stilted,
and also sometimes scary and right-wingish, and when you listen closely to these it's as if some warm pleasant fog suddenly
lifts and it strikes you that you're not at all sure it's John McCain
you want choosing the head of the EPA or the at least two new
justices who'll probably be coming onto the Supreme Court in
the next term, and you start wondering all over again what
makes the guy so attractive.[67]

While McCain is certainly capable of giving a good speech, the
question raised by this passage is why reporters should consider
the way McCain—or any candidate for that matter—acts "backstage" to be more important than the way he acts in more formal
settings or when he is talking to voters. The answer is, precisely
because the "backstage" is out of the public's view. This, supposedly, is where they can discern the "real" person behind the candidate. This is the place of privilege to which their press passes
grant them access, where the public is not admitted and true
insights can be gleaned. And this is where the most definitive
judgments—those that color how a candidate is presented in the
rest of the stories written about him—are made. This is where
John McCain rose and the likes of Gore, Dean, and Kerry fell. It
is not in the press conferences and speeches that McCain charmed
reporters and other candidates came off as too rehearsed or careful or ambitious or prickly. It was in the back of the plane, in the
van on the way to a fund-raiser, in the moments of downtime and
casual conversation where McCain's work was accomplished.
    While there is value in reporters offering a backstage glimpse

of the candidate, few could argue this excuses them of a respon-
sibility to discuss and analyze what that candidate offers "front-
stage" as well. What candidates do and say when the klieg lights
are on may be more self-conscious than what they do behind
the scenes, but it is still "real" in a fundamental way. The positions they take will be those on which they act once in office.
Despite popular belief, scholars have found that presidents keep
the vast majority of the promises they make on the campaign
trail.[68] Wallace's observations underscore what is notably missing
from the bulk of coverage about McCain: any serious analysis
of *what he actually thinks about issues.* A November 2006 op-ed in
the *Los Angeles Times* by Matt Welch set out to determine just that,
something in which his colleagues have been so strikingly uninter
ested:

> You can read 1,000 profiles of GOP presidential front-runner
> John McCain without encountering a single paragraph examin-
> ing his core ideological philosophy. His career is filled with
> such distracting drama—torture at the Hanoi Hilton, noisy
> conversion to the campaign-finance-reform faith, political sui-
> cide on the Straight Talk Express—that by the time you're
> done with the highlights, and perhaps a few "maverick" anec-
> dotes, time's up.
>
> People are forever filling in the blanks with their own polit-
> ical fantasies. Third party candidate! John Kerry running mate!
> Far-right warmonger! Republican In Name Only! But with the
> announcement that the popular Arizona senator has formed
> his presidential exploratory committee, it's time for our long
> national guessing game to end. . . .
>
> "Our greatness," he wrote in "Worth the Fighting For,"

"depends upon our patriotism, and our patriotism is hardly
encouraged when we cannot take pride in the highest public
institutions." So, because steroids might be damaging the faith
of young baseball fans, drug testing becomes a "transcendent
issue," requiring threats of federal intervention unless pro
sports leagues shape up. Hollywood's voluntary movie-rating
system? A "smoke screen to provide cover for immoral and
unconscionable business practices." Ultimate Fighting on Indian
reservations? "Barbaric" and worthy of government pressure on
cable TV companies. Negative political ads by citizen groups?
They "do little to further beneficial debate and healthy political
dialogue" and so must be banned for 60 days before an election
if they mention a candidate by name.

If his issues line up with yours, and if you're not overly concerned by an activist federal government, McCain can be a
great and sympathetic ally. But chances are he will eventually
see a grave national threat in what you consider harmless, or
he'll prescribe a remedy that you consider unconscionable.[69]

Welch may be right or wrong in his analysis of what drives
McCain's political philosophy. But his attempt to get beyond the
oft-told tales about McCain's biography and personality to a discussion of substance was, appearing as it did in one of the nation's
most important news outlets, nothing short of shocking. Arizona
reporters have been asking these kinds of questions for years—
wondering who the real John McCain is, looking beneath the
image to closely examine the substance, both what's good and
what's bad. But in the national press, explorations like the one
Welch undertook have been few and far between.

This is, of course, a weakness of political coverage of all presidential candidates, not just McCain. While reporters frequently

criticize candidates for being shallow, repeating talking points, or offering simplistic solutions to complex problems, seldom do they take the time to carefully examine the implications of the stances candidates do take. In the place of such substantive coverage, what we are left with is endless ruminations on "character," often vaguely defined and discussed through allegedly defining moments that usually have little if any real meaning. No candidate benefits more from this feature of political coverage than John McCain, whose character reporters long ago concluded is superior to that of all other politicians.

Chapter 2
Manufacturing McCain

In November 1982, John McCain won an open congressional seat in a heavily Republican district in Phoenix, Arizona. He had never run for office before. He also had been living in the state for less than two years. Yet despite his thin political résumé and tenuous ties to the people he sought to represent, McCain beat out other, more established Republicans to win the party nomination that would all but assure him a seat in Congress. His political career was off and running.

McCain's calling card, of course, was the dramatic and inspiring story of his captivity as a prisoner of war in Vietnam, from which he had returned less than a decade before. A combat pilot in the U.S. Navy, McCain came from a long line of military men.

His father was Admiral John Sidney McCain Jr., commander in chief of the U.S. Naval forces in the Pacific. His grandfather was Admiral John Sidney McCain Sr., who can be seen in the famous photograph of the Japanese surrender on the U.S.S. *Missouri* in 1945. McCain followed in their footsteps somewhat reluctantly. He was a poor student at Annapolis, finishing fifth from the bottom of the class. His youth was distinguished only by his carousing, which included all-night parties, Mediterranean jaunts, and whirlwind flings with beautiful women.[1]

But McCain eventually grew into the family tradition. In 1967, a matured McCain—now thirty years old, married, and with children—was deployed to Vietnam. On October 26, 1967, on a bombing run over Hanoi one month into his tour, McCain's plane was hit by a surface-to-air missile. As his Skyhawk spiraled downward, McCain managed to pull the ejector seat handle, but parachuted into a lake in the middle of Hanoi. With both arms and his right knee broken, McCain could hardly put up a fight when he was dragged onshore. McCain was held captive by the Vietnamese for the next five and a half years, a hellish period that saw him tortured, offered an early release (which he rejected), and forced into a false confession. When he was released in 1973, he was greeted as a hero, with a front-page photo in the *New York Times*.

For a brief moment following his return, McCain was a celebrity. In a lengthy article for *U.S. News & World Report*, McCain displayed an enthusiasm about his country that hit the right notes following the bitter feelings of the Vietnam era. "I think America today is a better country than the one I left nearly six years ago," he wrote. "I had a lot of time to think over there, and came to the conclusion that one of the most important things in life—along with a man's family—is to make some contribution to his country." As Robert Timberg, McCain's biographer, suggested, such statements "hinted at the politician to come." In the weeks that followed, McCain appeared in parades, delivered speeches, and became the object of public adulation.

Those days as a feted returning POW would also give him his first contact with Republican politics. In the spring of 1973, McCain was introduced to Ronald Reagan, who was then governor of California. The two men hit it off. Reagan admired McCain and enjoyed his company. For his part, McCain loved Reagan and considered him a political hero. Indeed, McCain would later describe Reagan's presidency as "the best thing that had happened to America in a long time."

By the late 1970s, however, McCain's period of glory was over. In 1977, McCain was appointed the Navy's Senate liaison, a good position if not necessarily a prestigious one. By then, it was becoming clear to McCain that his career in the Navy was nearing its end. His annual physical exams were not good, and he had not been assigned to a major sea command. It was around that time that he began thinking of a career in politics. As the Navy's liaison to the Senate, McCain cultivated relationships with powerful men on both sides of the political aisle, a move that would eventually pay off.[2]

If the story of his captivity in Vietnam was what made people notice John McCain, it was his second marriage that made his entrée into Arizona politics possible. In May 1980, McCain married Cindy Hensley, a beautiful southwestern belle who was seventeen years his junior. Hensley was the daughter of Jim Hensley, a Phoenix millionaire who at the time owned the largest Anheuser-Busch distributorship in the country.[3] The marriage took place a mere three months after McCain divorced his first wife, Carol. When asked why their marriage had failed, Carol McCain said, "I attribute it more to John turning forty and wanting to be twenty-five again than I do to anything else."[4]

Thus given an entrée into the Arizona elite, McCain went about plotting his new career. In early 1981, McCain met with J. Brian Smith, a Washington consultant who gave the Navy captain a primer in Arizona politics. Smith had been asked to meet with McCain by Senator Bill Cohen, a friend the two had in common— one of many connections that would reap benefits for the savvy McCain throughout his career. Over lunch, McCain told Smith that he was going to move to Arizona and run for Congress. McCain's scheme was simple: he would run for the new seat that the state would get in 1982 because of its growing population. He assumed that the seat would be in Phoenix, the Hensleys' base of power. The main stumbling block was that McCain would be running for a seat in a state barely a year and a half after taking up residence there—a blatant act of carpetbagging.

Before John and Cindy McCain moved to Arizona in March 1981, Smith advised McCain to remain mum about his political aspirations. "For God's sake, be very discreet," Smith told McCain. "It would be viewed as very opportunistic. Let's face it, it is, but let's not have it viewed that way," he added.[5] Once in state, McCain went schmoozing, attending luncheons and dinners where he introduced himself to Arizona's power elite. Jim Hensley also gave his son-in-law a public relations position that took him to conventions and meet and greets around the state. However, McCain's plan hit a snag when it was announced that Arizona's new congressional seat would be located in Tucson. With the Phoenix-area seats held by powerful incumbents, McCain's congressional aspirations seemed to have hit a wall.

But the state of limbo did not last long. In January 1982, in an incredible stroke of luck, Representative John Rhodes (R) announced that he was retiring. Rhodes held a seat in the First Congressional District, which included the Phoenix metro area.

The McCains lived just outside of the district—but that problem was soon solved. Later that day, Smith received a call from a jubilant McCain. As they discussed plans for a run, McCain asked someone in the room with him, "Did you buy it? Did you get it? Did you find it?" He got back on the line and told Smith that he had just been talking to his wife. "We just got a house in the First District," McCain told Smith.[6]

In the ensuing campaign, the hard-charging aspirant was plagued by accusations of carpetbagging. As Timberg wrote, McCain faced questions about how well he knew the district and charges of opportunism.[7] But McCain had the perfect retort. At a candidates' forum, responding to direct accusations of carpetbagging from an opponent, McCain sounded a now-familiar theme:

> Listen, pal. I spent twenty-two years in the Navy. My father was in the Navy. My grandfather was in the Navy. We in the military service tend to move a lot. We have to live in all parts of the country, all parts of the world. I wish I could have the luxury, like you, of growing up and living and spending my entire life in a nice place like the First District of Arizona, but I was doing other things.

Then, the coup de grace: "As a matter of fact, when I think about it now, the place I lived longest in my life was Hanoi."[8] The effect was devastating. The audience erupted in applause.

McCain defeated three other candidates to take the Republican nomination. The general election itself was just a formality, and the heavily Republican district made McCain its new congressman. In less than two years, John McCain had gone from being a Washington, DC–area resident, working inside the Beltway, to a representative for a district in Arizona.

A Bump in the Road

After just two terms in the House, McCain found the opportunity to move up when Senator Barry Goldwater retired in 1986. He was unopposed in the Republican primary and rolled to an easy general election win, defeating his opponent by twenty points. But he did not garner national attention until four years later, when he became known as one of the "Keating Five," senators caught up in one of the biggest financial scandals in American history.

Years later, McCain still stands untainted by the episode, which has now been reduced to a footnote in the story of the senator's career—"my asterisk," as McCain puts it.[9] But Keating Five was no mere asterisk. It was a major political scandal involving a wealthy campaign donor, compromised lawmakers, browbeaten regulators, and the biggest bank failure in U.S. history at the time. On the sidelines were thousands of retirees who saw their savings disappear into thin air, victims of a reckless and unscrupulous executive and the senators who coddled him.

John McCain was one of those senators. In April 1987, McCain, along with four of his colleagues, met with federal banking regulators at the behest of Charles Keating Jr., a wealthy Phoenix developer who ran Lincoln Savings and Loan, which was at the time under scrutiny by federal banking regulators for making risky investments with its depositors' funds. As part of Ronald Reagan's deregulatory spree in the 1980s, savings and loan associations, also known as thrifts, were given more leeway to invest depositor funds in commercial real estate. Many S&Ls proceeded to make speculative investments, drawing the scrutiny of federal regulators. When the real estate market crashed in the late 1980s, many S&Ls crashed along with it, leaving the taxpayers to pick up the tab.

Keating's Lincoln Savings and Loan was among the biggest speculators—and also the biggest of the flameouts. Charles Keating bought Lincoln in 1984 and went about transforming what had been a traditional thrift that made home loans into a hard-charging institution that took full advantage of the deregulated climate. Keating bought land and invested in risky securities and junk bonds. In 1985, the Federal Home Loan Bank Board took notice of the rise of aggressive thrifts and limited the amount of "direct investments" they could make in raw land, development, and high-risk bonds—a move that made the board and its head, Edwin Gray, a natural target of Keating. Keating was able to fend off pressure from regulators and continue running his company without fear of government intervention. But Keating's operation could only go on for so long. In 1989, Lincoln Savings and Loan collapsed. The ensuing bailout cost $2.6 billion in taxpayer funds, the largest of the S&L failures. In addition, seventeen thousand investors lost a total of $190 million.[10]

The investigations and reports that followed landed McCain and four other senators—Democrats Dennis DeConcini (AZ), Alan Cranston (CA), John Glenn (OH), and Donald Riegle Jr. (MI)—on the front page, their mug shots accompanied by dollar figures showing the amount Keating had raised for them over the years. Between 1982 and 1987, the five senators received a total of $1.4 million in campaign contributions and gifts from Keating.[11] Asked at a press conference if his contributions had bought him influence, Keating replied, "I want to say in the most forceful way I can: I certainly hope so."[12] It was revealed that the senators had met with regulators twice on Keating's behalf. The first meeting was held April 2, 1987, in DeConcini's office, and included

McCain, Glenn, Cranston, and DeConcini (Riegle did not attend). At that meeting, the senators requested that Gray withdraw the direct investment regulation in exchange for Lincoln cleaning up its act. Gray refused. He also told the senators that he did not have specific information about Lincoln, and that regulators in California would be better informed about Lincoln's situation. That led to a second meeting a week later between the five senators and regulators from the Federal Home Loan Bank of San Francisco and the Federal Savings and Loan Insurance Corp. According to William Black, the deputy director of the FSLIC, the senators "presented themselves as a group, and DeConcini is the dad, who's going to take the primary speaking role."[13] At the meeting, McCain stressed that Keating was a constituent and major employer in his state, though he added, "I wouldn't want any special favors for them." The regulators told the five senators that their investigations had concluded that Lincoln was acting recklessly, failing to perform credit reports on its borrowers and using federally insured deposits to make risky loans. One of them told the lawmakers that Lincoln was a "ticking time bomb." The regulators also informed the senators that they would be sending a criminal referral to the Department of Justice regarding Lincoln.

After the meeting, McCain said that he was done with Keating. "Again I was troubled by the appearance of the meeting," McCain told reporters later. "I stated I didn't want any special favors from them. I only wanted them to be fairly treated."[14] Black, however, was skeptical. In interviews after the scandal had blown over, he argued that if McCain had been really concerned about the appearance of impropriety, then he should not have shown up for the meetings at all. He told an *Arizona Republic* reporter that he believed that McCain attended them because he wanted to retain

Keating as a political sponsor. "Keating was incredibly powerful. And incredibly useful," said Black.[15]

In the wake of Lincoln's massive failure in the spring of 1989, news of the senators' meetings with regulators made national headlines. Gray testified that the senators' actions had been an effort to "subvert" the regulatory process. News reports and congressional hearings eventually showed that McCain's relationship with Keating was more involved than McCain had described. Keating was in fact a longtime friend of the Arizona senator's. The two men met in 1981 at a Navy League dinner in Arizona, and Keating raised money for McCain's 1982 and 1984 bids for the House and his 1986 run for the Senate.

But campaign contributions were not all of it. After his 1982 victory, McCain and his family made at least nine trips on Keating's dime, three of which were to Keating's own home in the Bahamas. McCain never disclosed the trips, as House rules required, until the scandal came out into the open in 1989. After the trips were publicized, McCain paid Keating $13,433 for travel expenses. In addition, McCain's wife and father-in-law were discovered to have invested $359,100 in a strip mall owned by Keating a year before McCain's meeting with regulators.[16] Cindy McCain and Jim Hensley would eventually reap between $100,000 and $1 million from the deal.[17] McCain was adamant that he "in 'no way abused" his office.[18]

In November 1990, the Senate Ethics Committee opened hearings to decide what punishment should be meted out to the Keating Five. The web of improprieties earned McCain a rebuke from the Senate committee, albeit a relatively minor one. In the end, McCain, along with Glenn, was found guilty of only "poor judgment." Meanwhile, the other three senators were found to have substantially interfered with regulatory efforts on behalf of

Keating. McCain's popularity in Arizona plummeted; one poll in January 1990 found only 33 percent of Arizonans rating him positively.[19]

Nonetheless, McCain considered himself exonerated by the ruling and contributed $112,000—the amount Keating raised for him—to the Treasury.[20] He also injected his own spin into the story line, arguing that he had been ensnared in the scandal because congressional Democrats needed at least one Republican to implicate in the mess—an explanation that seems to ignore the fact that McCain, as the *Economist* put it, "was the only one of the five who benefited personally" from Keating's largesse.[21] McCain's story also conveniently left out the fact that as a congressman he had sponsored legislation to delay new regulations limiting risky investments by S&Ls—legislation that benefited his friend Charles Keating.

In the years since, new revelations have filled out the picture of McCain's actions at the time. While the general consensus about McCain's involvement in the scandal has been that it was relatively benign, some have pointed out that McCain's expert handling of the situation and the press helped prevent graver damage to his career. According to a 2000 *Boston Globe* story, there is considerable evidence that McCain's office was the source of leaks to the press that proved to be favorable to McCain and undermined three of the four other senators, DeConcini, Cranston, and Riegle. According to one former McCain aide, the senator's media strategy as the scandal unfolded was "to create the clear impression he did little wrong, but that others had." In October 1989, McCain held a press conference to admit that he had made mistakes. At the same time, his office leaked a memo to the media that made DeConcini's role look more incriminating.[22] Another leak, following private testimony by McCain, led to an Associated

Press article headlined: "Source: Nothing New Found Against McCain."[23]

In 1992, McCain denied under oath that either he or his aides had anything to do with the leaks. However, in a 2000 interview, Clark B. Hall, who led the General Accounting Office probe of the Keating Five leaks, said that he had no doubt that McCain was one of the principal leakers. "You don't betray other people to protect yourself, and that's what he was doing," Hall said. "And he was breaking Senate rules to do it."[24] Peter Fleming Jr., a special counsel who conducted a later inquiry into the matter, did not directly implicate anyone, but found that circumstantial evidence made a compelling case that McCain's office was the source of some of the critical leaks. Those conclusions echoed those by Warren Rudman, cochairman of McCain's 2000 campaign and vice chairman of the Ethics Committee at the time of the scandal, who stated in a 1996 book that McCain and his staff were among those responsible for the leaks. For his part, DeConcini has said he is convinced that McCain was behind the leaks that made him look worse and McCain look better.

When confronted by the *Globe* in 2000 about the allegations, the McCain camp was furious. "The Bush campaign must be paying you for your time," was the response from John Dowd, a friend of McCain's. McCain himself was predictably angry. When interviewed by Hall, McCain reportedly snapped at the congressional investigator. "Senator McCain has a reputation as a stand-up guy, but his reaction that day was to point the finger at others," Hall said, calling McCain's reaction "contemptible" and "consistent with the leaks themselves, which were intended to shift the blame elsewhere."[25]

McCain's handling of the media during the Keating Five scandal showed hints of his evolving ability to master his public image and manipulate the press. Few people seem to recall these days that John McCain the senator was largely unknown until the Keating Five scandal erupted. Indeed, the first time most Americans learned John McCain's name, it was in connection with the most well-known piece of a scandal that eventually cost the taxpayers well over $100 billion.[26] But McCain's deft handling of the press when the scandal broke helped minimize the damage. Initially, McCain responded with rage. The *Arizona Republic* described what happened when the Keating Five scandal became public:

> When the story broke, McCain did nothing to help himself. When reporters first called him, he was furious. Caught out in the open, the former fighter pilot let go with a barrage of cover fire. Sen. Hothead came out in all his glory.
>
> "You're a liar," McCain snapped Sept. 29 when a *Republic* reporter asked him about business ties between his wife and Keating.
>
> "That's the spouse's involvement, you idiot," McCain said later in the same conversation. "You do understand English, don't you?"
>
> He also belittled the reporters when they asked about his wife's ties to Keating. "It's up to you to find that out, kids."
>
> And then he played the POW card.
>
> "Even the Vietnamese didn't question my ethics," McCain said.[27]

But as the *Republic* story noted, McCain later held a news conference and was "a changed man. He stood calmly for 90 minutes and answered every question."[28] Thereafter, McCain's strategy in dealing with the Keating Five scandal was to be accessible to any reporter who wanted to talk about it. As a *Washington Post* story at the time noted, McCain was "the most vocal of the five since the recent calls to investigate their conduct."[29] Bill Muller of the *Arizona Republic* noted, "McCain's hobnobbing with the press had an unexpected side effect. Reporters started to like him."[30] McCain also made sure to appear contrite, even as he attacked the Senate investigation as politically motivated. To this day, McCain plays the self-flagellating sinner when asked about the scandal. "I created the appearance of impropriety . . . five Senators meeting with regulators on behalf of a major contributor. I can't excuse it to you," he told one interviewer.[31] "The appearance of it was wrong," McCain said in 2000. "It's a wrong appearance when a group of senators appear in a meeting with a group of regulators, because it conveys the impression of undue and improper influence. And it was the wrong thing to do," he said at another time.[32] He has also been careful to stress that the Keating Five scandal was the "worst thing" that had ever happened to him,[33] a comment that, coming from a former POW, underscored the intensity of his penitence.

That one of the Keating Five could not only remain in office as long as McCain has, but flourish in the succeeding years, attests to the success of McCain's damage control efforts in the wake of the scandal and his skills as a politician. Of course, McCain had plenty of help from his friends in the press. Despite how big a story it was at the time, the Keating Five episode has been relegated to the status of footnote in the McCain narrative. "The interesting thing to me is that he doesn't seem to carry any taint of the Keating Five," said Ben Scheffner, a reporter for *Roll Call*, in a 1997 interview.[34] Indeed, a search of major newspapers turns up less than two dozen mentions of the Keating Five scandal in connection with McCain since the beginning of 2003.[35] And when it does come up, it is usually reduced to a sentence or two, and in redemptive terms—as the incident that sparked the senator's fervor for campaign finance reform.

Torie Clarke, McCain's former press secretary, called Keating Five a turning point for John McCain. "People get inspired to do great things by bad things," she said. "In many ways being a POW was the best thing that happened to him as a person. And Keating was the best thing to happen to him as a public servant."[36] Without McCain's increasingly friendly relations with the reporters who would choose when and how to discuss the scandal, it seems unlikely that it would have done so little lasting damage to his image. In the end, they proved more than willing to repeat this road-to-Damascus interpretation of the scandal. In a fawning 2005 profile in the *New Yorker*, Connie Bruck wrote that out of the humiliation of the incident McCain "took lessons that came to define him as a very different kind of politician." The experience helped McCain develop "an intense aversion to partisanship." It also inspired him to "remake the system that encouraged such transgressions."[37]

It was hardly the first time this story had been told. "Prison shaped his character," read the subtitle to a glowing *Time* magazine portrait in December 1999. "Scandal shaped his crusade."[38] "McCain learned from his mistakes, and then some. He became a tireless crusader against the nefarious influence of big money on the political system. He violated Republican orthodoxy by fighting for campaign finance reform and taking on the tobacco industry. He became a favorite of jaded journalists because he is one of the few politicians who will say exactly what's on his mind, damned be the consequences," wrote syndicated columnists Jack Anderson and Jan Moller.[39] The scandal, wrote the *Orlando Sentinel*, "drove McCain to oppose the wishes of Republican leaders and become a national crusader for reforming what he saw as a corrupt campaign-finance system."[40] Afterward, wrote conservative columnist Debra Saunders, "McCain, the least culpable and most repentant of the unfab five, committed himself to rid politics of the taint of bad money."[41] "It was the 'Keating Five' experience which seared his soul and which turned him into a campaign finance reformer," said NBC's Andrea Mitchell.[42] Like George W. Bush's struggles with alcohol, the Keating Five story was a negative that McCain managed to turn into a positive, a story of long-ago sin redeemed.

This is not to say that McCain's desire for campaign finance reform was offered disingenuously. But what is notable about it is how consistently the press situates the issue in precisely the narrative that McCain would want, one that not only forgives and redeems his prior sins, but paints the man as he is today in just the way he attempts to position himself politically.

Making the Maverick

Perhaps no word better defines John McCain in the public imagination than "maverick." It's a word that, more than "straight talk" or "moderate" or "reformer," has come to occupy a seemingly permanent place next to the senator's name in the media. It is also distinct from those other modifiers that have come to identify McCain. As critical as the idea of ideological moderation is to the Myth of McCain, his status as a maverick is not about what he believes but about who he is—something far more important in the personality-driven world of today's politics.

In later years, when asked to name his proudest moment in Congress, John McCain would go all the way back to his first year in the House of Representatives to point to a case in which he stood against a Republican president. In 1983, McCain voted against Ronald Reagan's decision to deploy U.S. troops to Lebanon. "I do not see any obtainable objectives in Lebanon," he said at the time, "and the longer we stay there, the harder it will be to leave."[43] McCain sees the act as a defining moment: the neophyte lawmaker breaking ranks with his party and his political hero. (The actual vote was 270–161 in favor of deployment; McCain was joined by twenty-seven Republicans in opposition.) The dissenters would later be vindicated when a truck bomber slammed into the Marine barracks in Lebanon, killing 241 U.S. servicemen and precipitating a U.S. withdrawal. "It demonstrated to me that you really have to do, at the end of the day, what you fundamentally know is right," McCain told the *National Journal* years later.[44]

At the time, McCain's decision to object was barely noted (a *New York Times* story on the House vote buried a quote from him at the bottom of its story). McCain evidently sees his 1983 vote as the moment where his political identity as a maverick began to form, but that reputation did not really take hold until much later. In fact, McCain's early years in Congress did not attract much national attention, nor did they evince much evidence of what would become the Myth of McCain. It wasn't until the late 1980s that the press even began to take notice of his self-proclaimed penchant for breaking with party orthodoxy. Early in his career, McCain was seldom described as someone too principled to be bound by party loyalty or the momentary dictates of partisanship. The first time anyone referred to him as a "maverick" in the press appears to be a February 1989 States News Service story, which quoted Dan Casey, then–executive director of the American Conservative Union, saying about McCain, "He is a good conservative but somewhat of a maverick."[45] There was no explanation of what made him a maverick, other than the fact that the group had given him a rating of merely 80 out of 100. Other such descriptions are few and far between. Another story from 1989, in *Newsday*, described him as a Republican expected to "break ranks" on Dick Cheney's proposed budget cuts to the F-14D aircraft program.[46] But apart from these faint glimmers, there was little indication of the McCain image that would eventually form in the press.

In 1992, McCain was one of three Republican senators to vote for Democratic campaign finance reform legislation (all the Senate Democrats except two voted in favor). The bill called for the provision of taxpayer funds and other incentives to urge candidates to abide by voluntary spending limits; it was vetoed by then-president George H. W. Bush, a veto that the Senate failed to override. In 1993, McCain again cast himself in the role of party rebel in the campaign finance debate. In deliberations over an identical measure to the one Bush had vetoed in 1992, McCain proposed amendments that caught the attention of the media. McCain offered one amendment that barred candidates from using campaign money for personal expenses such as vacations, mortgage payments, and clothing purchases, among others. Another amendment pushed for the campaign reforms, if enacted, to go into effect in 1994 instead of 1996, as originally proposed. Little noted was that McCain's amendment was identical to one that his Arizona colleague, Senator Dennis DeConcini (D), was set to introduce to the Senate, before McCain beat him to the punch by a day—a move that won McCain credit for the amendment.[47]

The early returns to these maneuvers were encouraging. In 1993, the *Washington Post* noted that McCain was one of five "maverick" Republicans for his work on campaign finance reform legislation.[48] Another *Post* reference two months later offered a continuation of the theme, describing McCain as a "conservative with maverick instincts."[49] But if the media had taken a closer look, talk of McCain as a maverick may have been a little premature. As news stories at the time made clear, the 1992 campaign finance bill was preordained to be vetoed by Bush, making it easier for McCain and his fellow Republican rebels to back it. That motive became starker in 1993 when the Clinton administration, pushing a nearly identical bill, was told by McCain and his fellow "renegades" that they would support a Republican filibuster of the legislation. Predictably, Clinton expressed his dismay at the "rebels" who changed their tune when faced with a bill that might actually become law. "The thing that particularly troubles me about this one is that several Republicans voted for a bill not unlike this last year which contained public financing," Clinton said. The Associated Press reported that Republican moderates admitted to voting for the original bill only because they knew it would be vetoed.[50] Eventually, McCain and his band of mavericks broke with their GOP colleagues on the filibuster, but only after the bill was gutted to remove most of the public financing features of the measure. The compromise legislation "left almost no one happy" and was derided by advocacy groups like Public Citizen and US PIRG as watered down.[51] The bill eventually died a quiet death in the House. McCain's maverick gestures, though revealed to be less than substantial under scrutiny, nonetheless left their imprint on the media.

In addition to his campaign finance stance, McCain also made some moves during the period that helped gain the attention of political observers and move the maverick theme forward. In 1993, McCain publicly offered to accompany President Bill Clinton to the Vietnam Veterans Memorial on Memorial Day, providing cover for the president, who had been warned by veterans' groups angry with his failure to serve in the war to stay away from the monument. Later that year, McCain, working with Senate Democrat (and fellow Vietnam veteran) John Kerry, urged Clinton to lift U.S. trade sanctions against Vietnam. In 1994, McCain and Kerry sponsored a resolution to lift the embargo, against the opposition of veterans' groups and prominent Republican senators like Bob Dole and Phil Gramm. The two would continue to work with the president to accelerate the normalization of trade relations with the country.

In 1995, the *National Journal*, the Washington insider's bible, published a profile of McCain simply titled "The Maverick." It was the first of what would be a cascade of glowing profiles to come, many of which would center on McCain's penchant for unpredictability and rebelliousness. The article, by James Kitfield, led with an anecdote of a McCain outburst in front of the reporter about the way the GOP's conservative wing had spoken out against Colin Powell as a possible presidential candidate. Conservative activists within the GOP deemed Powell insufficiently ideological for the Republican revolution then sweeping Washington. Talking to Kitfield, McCain assailed the hard-liners in the GOP who targeted Powell. "Politics can be a very cruel business because there are people out there like [conservative activist] Paul Weyrich, who has never stood up for public office and thus has never had to answer to the public, yet who feels free to indulge in character assassination," McCain said. He also expressed doubts about the health of his party: "Certainly for conservatives to attack [Powell's] character in the ad hominem fashion they did makes me believe we do have some problems within our party."[52]

Such a demonstrative display against members of his own party seemed to confirm what a handful of other examples had hinted at: that McCain was that rare thing, a true independent.

The *Journal* profile fixed on his support for normalizing Vietnam relations, outreach to Bill Clinton over the Vietnam Memorial brouhaha, and opposition to pork in defense budgets as examples of the maverick at work. Kitfield also found a Democratic Senate aide to bolster the impression: "[McCain is] also interesting in that even when you wage battle with him, you usually find some middle ground. In that sense, he's put himself somewhat in the role of an honest broker in the Republican Caucus."[53] For his part, McCain went to his old standby—his POW experience—to build on the emerging theme. "My refusal of early release [in Vietnam] gave me a confidence in my own judgment," he said, adding, "That event gave me confidence that once I've examined something, I know what's right, and I'm willing to hold that position even when it doesn't receive the approval of my colleagues in the short run."[54]

The mid-nineties saw McCain edging closer to the national spotlight. In 1995, Robert Timberg's *A Nightingale's Song*, an unabashed valentine to the Arizona senator, was published. The book traced the trajectories of five U.S. Naval Academy graduates—McCain, Oliver North, Robert McFarlane, John Poindexter, and James Webb—whose experiences summed up the nation's own painful experience in Vietnam. In 1996, McCain received some attention as a potential vice presidential candidate for Dole, who at the time was the American politician most known for being a military veteran. Aware of the buzz beginning to grow for McCain, the party chose him as the keynote speaker at the Republican National Convention. The performance, in which he discussed his captivity in Vietnam, was a hit. William Safire, writing in the *New York Times*, called it a "brief gem from a brave man," a speech "delivered with quiet modesty and grace."[55] Other plaudits soon followed. In 1997, *Time* magazine named McCain one of

America's twenty-five most influential people, citing his campaign finance reform work and willingness to anger party colleagues.[56]

Before running for president, McCain found one more issue on which to make a public break with his party—if only briefly—and win praise from the press. In November 1997, McCain introduced a bill to provide the Food and Drug Administration with a number of new regulatory powers over tobacco products, in order to "reform and restructure the processes by which tobacco products are manufactured, marketed, and distributed."[57] Giving the FDA the power to regulate tobacco would have been a significant change in policy—one that his Republican colleagues, who receive millions in contributions from tobacco companies, were none too eager to see enacted. After a long process of amendments to the bill, it was eventually killed by Senate Republicans in June 1998.

Reporters quickly wedded the tobacco bill to the campaign finance issue, often mentioning the two issues as a pair proving McCain's maverick tendencies. Meanwhile, some commentators began to notice. "The Senator is cherished by journalists for his quixotic fights on campaign finance reform and tobacco, his scorn for pols driven by polls or pork, and his loose tongue," wrote New York Times columnist Maureen Dowd in 1999.[58] "Many reporters loved his Senate crusade against the tobacco companies and publicly cheered on his campaign finance reform efforts. They are addicted to the McCain phenomenon," wrote Charlie Cook of the National Journal after McCain's campaign ended in 2000.[59] Again and again, even years later, the tobacco legislation is brought up as an example of how McCain goes his own way, whatever the political consequences.

That continues to be the case, despite the fact that in the decade since McCain's bill died in 1998, he has done *nothing* to press the issue further. He did not reintroduce the bill, nor did he attempt to introduce a modified version. If you believe that tobacco should be regulated by the FDA, McCain's effort in 1997 was ineffectual, and he has been absent from the issue ever since. But it did accomplish something significant—for McCain's image.

The Maverick Goes National

On December 30, 1998, John McCain filed his candidacy papers for his presidential campaign. Within a matter of months, McCain the maverick would explode out of the Beltway and become a national brand.

The January 14, 1999, edition of the Capitol Hill newspaper *Roll Call* featured an article laying out the utility of McCain's image to a bid for higher office: "Reputation as Maverick Could Benefit McCain in 2000 Presidential Bid."[60] The Associated Press picked up on the theme four days later, juxtaposing his "Ronald Reagan conservatism" with his "maverick image." The story cited McCain's "largely scandal-free past," as though the Keating Five scandal had never happened.[61]

The "invisible primary"—the period when few other than political junkies are paying attention to the nascent campaign— was barely under way before the arbiters of conventional wisdom followed suit. The "maverick" label appeared in story after story. *Time*'s Margaret Carlson wrote of the "maverick McCain."[62] Mary McGrory of the *Washington Post* hailed him as the "Arizona maverick."[63] William Safire, in his *New York Times* column, called McCain a "genuine maverick" with appeal to independent voters.[64] What's noteworthy about these stories is that they referred to McCain as a maverick without providing a single example or citation to explain exactly what made him so—not even bothering to mention campaign finance reform or tobacco. McCain's maverick standing was simply noted, with the assumption that readers would know what the commentator was talking about.

CNN in particular was an instrumental contributor to building the maverick image. In 1999, CNN aired more stories describing McCain as a "maverick" than any other broadcast or cable news network. CNN in all aired thirty-seven stories that featured McCain as a maverick, compared with Fox's nine and MSNBC's three.[65] CNN also topped CBS, NBC, and ABC, which had eight, three, and one stories respectively that defined McCain as a maverick. On an April 1999 episode of *Inside Politics*, political analyst William Schneider said, "McCain's been called a moderate by some for his stands on tobacco and campaign finance reform. Is he a moderate, a curse word for many conservatives? No, he's a maverick."[66] In a broadcast a few months later, Wolf Blitzer said that McCain had "gained the reputation as a maverick within the Republican Party."[67] By the second half of 1999, McCain the maverick was an established theme. In September, CNN's Candy Crowley noted the trend: "The word used most often to describe the politics of John McCain is 'maverick.'"[68] In November, Bob Garfield stated that McCain was "unafraid" to be "kind of a maverick."[69] On *Crossfire*, liberal cohost Bill Press joined in the chorus, claiming that McCain had "a well-deserved reputation as a maverick."[70]

By the time the battle for the New Hampshire primaries heated up in December 1999, McCain's insurgent campaign had become established as the favorite—not among Republican primary voters, but among the national media. The *New York Times*, in a December 30, 1999, profile, dubbed McCain an "anti-politician."[71] On the day of the New Hampshire primary, the *Times* affixed the subhead "The Maverick" to its story on the McCain campaign.

On this wave of positive coverage, it was unsurprising that national polls showed McCain gaining traction with the public at large. In a June 1999 *Washington Post* poll of Republicans and Republican leaners nationwide, 49 percent said they would vote for Bush as their nominee, while 20 percent said they would choose Elizabeth Dole. McCain came in a distant third, tied at 5 percent with Pat Buchanan.[72] McCain's status would improve dramatically in the coming months, however. In an ABC News/ *Washington Post* poll released February 28, 2000, McCain towered over the Republican and Democratic fields with a 60 percent favorability rating (Gore was second with 50 percent).[73] Perhaps reflective of the fawning media coverage, McCain also topped Bush and Gore on another question: "The more I hear about (Gore/Bush/McCain) the more I like him . . ." By that likeability measure, McCain got 54 percent, compared with 44 percent and 41 percent for Bush and Gore, respectively. The responses to another question, which asked respondents whether they believed a candidate "says what he really thinks, even if it's not politically popular," suggested that the maverick image was beginning to stick. McCain easily won that question too, with 67 percent of respondents saying "yes," compared with Bush and Gore's 53 percent and 41 percent, respectively. That marked a sharp increase for McCain from a December 1999 ABC News/*Washington Post* poll, when only 52 percent of respondents said "yes" for McCain, while Bush and Gore received 57 percent and 43 percent, respectively.

Despite the Bush campaign's overwhelming financial and organizational strength, McCain went on to win New Hampshire, upsetting the presumptive favorite. It was in the wake of his surprising success in New Hampshire that McCain became the top political story in the country. *Time* magazine hailed "The McCain Mutiny" on its cover, portraying McCain as an anti-establishment rebel (two months earlier, their cover featured "The Real McCain," with the subtitle, "His heroic life story and passion for reform could give Bush a run for his money"). One scholarly study examining the effects of media coverage during the 2000 primaries found that the more Republican primary voters paid attention to the news, the more likely they were to support McCain, particularly after New Hampshire:

> When media favoritism was moderately favorable (before New Hampshire), we see marginal effects. But after media coverage toward McCain's candidacy became overwhelmingly favorable at the expense of Bush, respondents who paid attention to this coverage were substantially influenced as a result. In other words, these results suggest that media favoritism played an instrumental role in creating the surge of momentum from which the McCain campaign benefited. Meanwhile, on the other side of the political spectrum, media reception appears to have played no meaningful role in shaping Democratic candidate evaluations, either before or after New Hampshire.[74]

In other words, the amount of news voters paid attention to had no impact on their feelings toward Al Gore and Bill Bradley. But the more news they got about the campaign, the more they liked John McCain. While such clear, short-term effects are unusual in media studies, this study seems to show that the positive press coverage McCain received led directly to more votes.

Looking at the surge of McCain stories from 1999 through the first months of 2000, it's not unfair to suggest that the "maverick" label was as much a creation of the peculiar groupthink that grips journalists during campaign season as it was a product of original reporting. For the political press corps, a snowball effect set in. While many stories routinely talked of McCain as a maverick, only a fraction of them offered any context or justification for the characterization, such as a list of votes or other factors to explain what exactly it was that made him a maverick. Those that did were more likely to drop in a reference to campaign finance reform without exploring it in any detail. Many stories were content simply to refer to McCain as a maverick—and leave it at that.

As E. R. Shipp, who was the *Washington Post*'s ombudsman, wrote at the time, her paper seemed to have assigned each of the major candidates a role and found itself unable or unwilling to look beyond the conclusions it had made: "Gore is the guy in search of an identity; Bradley is the Zen-like intellectual in search of a political strategy; McCain is the war hero who speaks off the cuff and is, thus, a 'maverick'; and Bush is a lightweight with a famous name, and has the blessings of the party establishment and lots of money in his war chest. As a result of this approach, some candidates are whipping boys; others seem to get a free pass."[75] Her description applied not just to the *Post* but to virtually the entire political press corps.

Although it emerged full-blown during the 2000 campaign, the maverick theme has remained a staple of McCain's coverage. Virtually every day—sometimes many times a day—a reporter or commentator somewhere in the American media is calling John McCain a maverick. Sometimes a reporter almost forgets to mention that McCain is a maverick, then catches him or herself, as NBC's Norah O'Donnell did when guest-hosting *Hardball* in June 2006. "All right, Senator John McCain—the maverick McCain," she said, ending their interview. Both laughed knowingly.[76]

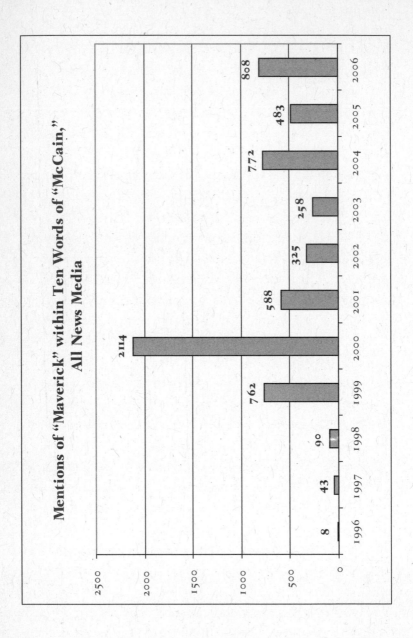

Mentions of "Maverick" within Ten Words of "McCain,"
All News Media

Hero Worship

John McCain's victory in New Hampshire turned out to be the peak of his 2000 candidacy. Three weeks later, he and his rival locked horns again in South Carolina. This time, Bush won decisively. The defeat all but spelled the end of McCain's run for the presidency. But even as the Straight Talk Express stalled on its way to the White House, McCain did not find himself abandoned by the media. On the contrary, McCain's loss only seemed to deepen the affection the nation's journalists felt for their favorite politician. This feeling was enhanced by the particular way he lost. In South Carolina, McCain was the target of a relentlessly negative, personal campaign. One reported tactic used against McCain was "push-polling" suggesting that McCain had fathered an illegitimate black child (the McCains have an adopted daughter from Bangladesh); another smear had its start in an e-mail by a Bob Jones University professor alleging that McCain had had children out of wedlock.

Everybody loves a winner, and the media are no different. In covering the political scene, journalists largely dispense with niggling questions of substance and value—questions that also happen to hold the most importance for the electorate. Instead, the media devotes an inordinate amount of time and space to questions of strategy. Who beat whom? Who's up and who's down? The wisdom of a particular policy and the veracity of its purported effects become less relevant in such circumstances; all that matters is that one player outfoxes another and wins the game.

When it came to John McCain, however, the media suddenly found itself rooting for the loser. Instead of raving about the no-holds-barred brilliance of Karl Rove's South Carolina campaign, which revived Bush's momentum and halted his opponent's, reporters wrote denunciations of the tactics used by the Bush campaign and its South Carolina supporters, alongside virtually tear-stained tributes to their fallen hero, one more good man felled by the harsh realities of politics. While Bush had received positive coverage up to that point and would be the beneficiary of a press corps that savaged his general election opponent mercilessly (as *Slate*'s Mickey Kaus wrote at the time about reporters, "They hate Gore. They really do think he's a liar. And a phony"[77]), this was the one moment during 2000 in which Bush could reasonably claim that the press was not on his side.

The McCain campaign's demise was met by the journalistic equivalent of a twenty-one-gun salute. Journalists could barely keep their disappointment hidden. In an interview with then syndicated radio host Don Imus, *Newsweek*'s Jonathan Alter admitted that it was "hard for us to cover" the campaign with the vicious attacks being heaped on McCain by Bush's team. Imus later said that Alter "sounded like he was going to slit his wrists."[78] Jacob Weisberg, writing in *Slate*, said that even though he had harbored "grave doubts" about whether McCain would be a good president (without saying what they were), he admitted that he was "disappointed" by McCain's loss, since "McCain challenged all that is hidebound, joyless, and mind-numbing in American campaigns."[79]

Particularly noteworthy were the tributes that painted the McCain loss in fatalistic terms, seeing it as an inevitable, even fitting, end to an idealistic campaign. Following the South Carolina debacle, Alter waxed philosophical: "Great suffering can ennoble, especially if the survivor emerges with his sense of humor. Reform crusades are about cleaning the system of its toxins."[80] A profile in the *New Republic* following the South Carolina defeat opened with an anecdote about McCain's stunning win in New

Hampshire. After CNN declared victory for McCain, everyone in his hotel room erupted—everyone except McCain. "It was the oddest thing," recalled one reporter in the room. "He looked as if he were watching his own funeral."[81] Later on, after the South Carolina rout, McCain "seemed almost joyful." The article suggested that such responses were "a glimpse of the true John McCain," a politician who "seems more comfortable losing."[82] Such readings put forward a variant of the McCain-as-maverick trope, painting McCain as a tragic hero, championing quixotic crusades at the expense of his own political success.

And so it was that the McCain-media love affair continued well after the 2000 election. Even as Bush was taking power, the press provided his primary rival a platform no other politician enjoyed. On the night Al Gore conceded the disputed 2000 election, McCain made the rounds on all the TV networks, talking about *his* plans. "Well, I want to work with Governor Bush on issues that are important to him. I hope that he will work on this issue that is important to me in a pledge I made to millions of Americans," McCain told Dan Rather.[83] On CNN, McCain thundered, "To say that we shouldn't take [campaign finance reform] up right after the inauguration because of some legislative agenda is simply nonsense."[84] Instead of framing McCain's comments as sour grapes from a sore loser—a fate Gore and Kerry suffered whenever they criticized the president in the wake of their losses—the media portrayed McCain's grandstanding as the continuation of his noble crusade.

McCain himself did his best to keep his agenda alive, talking of his "mandate" (begging the question, since when does a politician earn a mandate from losing a primary?) and dangling the possibility of defection to the Democratic Party. David Corn, writing in the *Nation*, took note of the press hysteria over McCain that hardly died down after the primaries: "Look, McCain is hosting Tom Daschle at his weekend home in Arizona! Is he about to bolt the GOP? McCain pals, including pundit/publisher/political strategist William Kristol, are meeting to ponder the possibilities of an independent McCain presidential run! Slap the news on the front page!"[85]

The image of McCain as Don Quixote, a valiant warrior fighting against the Republican establishment, the corrupt "system," and the militant base, was only burnished by the criticism of McCain by some high-profile conservatives. For a variety of reasons, in the 2000 primaries many conservatives had decided that George W. Bush was their man and John McCain couldn't be trusted. The National Right to Life Committee, for instance, opposed the McCain-Feingold legislation, fearing that it could curtail their political activities (the organization argued in 1998 that McCain-Feingold "could cripple the pro-life movement in the United States"[86]). They not only endorsed Bush, they ran ads attacking McCain—despite the fact that the two candidates' positions on abortion were essentially identical. During the primaries, conservative periodicals like the *American Spectator*, *Human Events* (a hard-right magazine that claims McCain as a reader),[87] and the *National Review* plugged hard for Bush and attacked McCain at every turn. That kind of treatment at the hands of the right only endeared him more to the mainstream media by helping to convince them that he was indeed an independent maverick, which in turn intensified the skepticism of McCain among some on the right. It was a feedback loop that enhanced his reputation as a moderate and an independent, unbeholden to any partisan line or ideological dogma.

What's noteworthy about the conservative animus toward McCain was that it was unusually obsessed with his positive mainstream press. To be sure, there were substantive reasons for the hard right's suspicions—campaign finance reform and his smaller tax cut compared with George W. Bush's, in particular—but the fixation on the relationship between the press and McCain was what many conservatives pointed to when criticizing McCain. Writing in the *National Review* in the heat of the primaries in May 2000, Ramesh Ponnuru conceded that the press actually had given Bush great coverage months earlier. However, that changed when McCain became a factor in the race. "The most important reason reporters have turned on Bush, of course, is that he's now taking on their hero," Ponnuru opined, decrying the free ride that McCain was getting from the media.[88] David Keene, head of the American Conservative Union, identified the problem many conservatives had with McCain. "He decided the media was his constituency, not conservatives, and he ran by attacking his own party. A lot of people decided then he couldn't be trusted," he said.[89]

But any cursory look at McCain's platform and voting record would tell you that conservatives need not have worried about a McCain presidency. The differences between him and Bush on policy issues were tiny; what defined the distinct roles they took on during the campaign were the choices each made. Bush undertook a carefully planned effort to become the GOP's establishment candidate, bringing prominent Republicans down to Texas to get to know him and courting key fund-raisers and political operatives. In response, McCain played the anti-establishmentarian role, something that underdogs running against presumptive favorites have done since time immemorial (and something that had gone over well in New Hampshire in the past).[90] Running as the insurgent gave McCain's campaign needed life but led, unsurprisingly, to his rejection by the Republican establishment, and he met the same fate as most underdogs. (Not all conservatives turned their back on McCain, however. The neoconservatives at the *Weekly Standard*, led by editor William Kristol; conservative icon Norman Podhoretz; columnists such as the *New York Times*'s David Brooks and the *Wall Street Journal*'s Dorothy Rabinowitz; and television pundit Tucker Carlson were among McCain's high-profile conservative allies. It's worth noting that they saw what many in the conservative camp overlooked—McCain's domestic right-wing bona fides, combined with his neoconservative vision of American foreign policy.)

In the wake of the primaries, Grover Norquist wrote, "McCain's not so secret weapon was the uncritical and unflagging support of the establishment media corporations. . . . The major media amplified McCain's message, muted Bush's, and found Republican quislings to quote against the conservative movement."[91] What Norquist did not mention was that on a whole host of issues— abortion, taxes, spending—McCain was actually not that distant from the hard-liners' choice, George W. Bush. The deal breaker for Norquist and his ilk was campaign finance reform. As one of the architects of the "K Street Project," a strategy aimed at enlisting Washington's business lobbies and PACs in the Republican revolution, Norquist had an understandable interest in keeping as much money *in* politics as possible. McCain's campaign reform legislation was thought by many at the time to pose a threat to Norquist's plan (though in fact it did little if anything to diminish the power of special interests). More important, a Bush presidency, with its close ties to business, promised to deepen and expand the K Street Project. As John Judis noted, "Norquist, [Majority Leader Tom] DeLay, and other conservative strategists . . . reduced conservatism to support for their fund-raising agenda."[92]

Less about McCain than about the nature of the conservative movement, the right-wing opposition to the Arizona senator nonetheless made the "maverick" irresistible to the media. To many in the establishment press, the Right's displeasure with McCain was enough to qualify him as, if not an outright liberal, then certainly a moderate. And to many conservatives, the media's infatuation with McCain was proof positive that he must in fact be a liberal. After all, if you believe that the media have an irredeemable liberal bias, and their affection for McCain is obvious, then how could he be anything but a liberal? This was the logic that led many conservatives to permanent suspicion of McCain. This suspicion only fed reporters' admiration for McCain, which in turn heightened conservatives' antipathy for him, and around the cycle went.

Though he had lost the election, McCain had become a central figure in American politics, sought out for quotes and interviews (in contrast to the fate of most presidential also-rans). By the time the 2004 presidential campaign rolled around, McCain had solidified his position atop the American political media landscape. With the election approaching and the partisan divide seemingly growing, the press repeatedly portrayed McCain as the one man in America who transcended ideology and party. "In a world currently divided into hostile Democratic and Republican planets, he's spun off on an orbit all his own," wrote the *New York Times*.[93]

Grover Norquist once compared McCain's strategy to "Madonna's business plan: He always has to do something new to get himself back on the cover of magazines."[94] Campaigning enthusiastically for Bush, McCain nonetheless bestowed compliments on his "friend" John Kerry. By the time of the Republican National Convention in New York City, McCain was a name invoked by both Bush and Kerry. "If there has ever been a time

when the same officeholder has been pictured and cited in ads by
both major-party candidates, I cannot remember it," wrote David
Broder.[95] *Newsweek*, in its pre-convention issue, dubbed McCain
"The Man in the Middle" for being so in demand by both campaigns.[96] Certainly, the image projected by the media was of a senator who was independent and towered over the petty politicking
of a presidential campaign. Yet four weeks after Broder's column,
the National Republican Senatorial Committee named McCain
"Team Player of the Week."[97] Few who saw the enthusiasm
with which he campaigned for Bush could doubt which team he
was on.

Special Treatment

The true extent of McCain's hallowed place among the nation's
scribes can be better appreciated when we look at how the media
has covered other recent presidential candidates. In 2000, McCain
was the beneficiary of what one could argue was the most fawning coverage of any presidential candidate in modern times. High-
lighting his strengths and obscuring his weaknesses, the media
created a sparkling image of McCain—in stark contrast to the
dark and derisive pictures they drew of other high-profile candidates.

For decades, conservatives have perpetuated the myth of a liberal media. While a whole book could be devoted to dismantling
that particular conservative shibboleth, suffice it to say that it
would be difficult to argue with a straight face that candidates like
Al Gore and John Kerry were beneficiaries of some media con-
spiracy to boost their campaigns. Kerry, for instance, faced a press
that eagerly used his opponent's spin to frame their own stories.
Did Kerry throw away his Vietnam medals in protest of the war?

Did he lie to get his medals to begin with? How badly is his flip-flopping going to hurt him? And just how out of touch and aloof is he? Never mind that Bush and Cheney had taken a pass on serving in Vietnam, or that Bush had his own share of reversals on policy issues, or that he had known no other existence but a life of privilege insulated from the concerns of the average joe. While McCain was never criticized for building his 2000 campaign on his Vietnam history, Kerry was said to have made too much of his. At times the media coverage of Kerry—fixated on trivia like his wife's temper, or his valet, or his snowboarding—got so hostile that it left *conservative* commentators bewildered. "There's an amazing media piling-on here that I'm quite surprised at, frankly," said conservative pundit Cal Thomas at one point on *Fox News Watch*. When even Fox commentators note the unfairness of media coverage toward a Democrat, then you know something is amiss.[98]

Something similar happened to Howard Dean. For years, McCain has gotten away with being an intemperate grouch because the media simply refuses to portray him as one. (See the next chapter.) In 2004, the same media that had given McCain a pass characterized Howard Dean as "angry," culminating in the ridiculously overblown attention given to "The Scream" the night of the Iowa caucuses. Dean's enthusiastic whooping, amplified by the video and audio coverage that muffled the noise of the auditorium, quickly became a defining event, crystallizing for the media all that was wrong with the angry, ill-tempered, and radical Dean. Within days it was replayed hundreds of times on television and radio. The fact that Dean also claimed to want to clean up a corrupt Washington, and drew opposition from establishment figures in his own party, ultimately did little to get the press on his side.

As for Al Gore, he faced a press corps as unremittingly hostile to him as they were friendly to McCain. If McCain came to represent everything reporters wanted politicians to be, Gore was portrayed as the embodiment of everything reporters dislike: ambitious, calculated, careful, and above all, dishonest. In order to paint this picture, they propagated a series of false stories about Gore—some at the urging of the Bush campaign, and some that they simply invented on their own—including the claims that Gore said he had grown up on a farm, was the inspiration for the lead character in *Love Story*, and discovered the existence of toxic waste at Love Canal. In every case, Gore did not say what the press said he said, and in every case, the press ran with the story of Gore's alleged dishonesty with undisguised excitement. No lie was spread farther and wider than this one: "Al Gore said he invented the Internet." If you were alive in 2000, you heard this claim; it appeared in over a thousand stories in the American media during the campaign. But what you probably don't know is that *Al Gore never said he invented the Internet*. What he actually said was, "During my service in the United States Congress, I took the initiative in creating the Internet"—plainly a statement about his work as a congressman on the Internet, and not a claim that he had "invented" anything. And it was true, to boot. During the 1980s, when the Internet was little more than a network linking a few universities, Gore repeatedly advocated greater funding for computer networking research. Among the bills he later introduced were the High Performance Computing and Communication Act of 1991, which led to the development of the first Web browser, and the Information Infrastructure and Technology Act of 1992, which opened the Internet to commercial traffic.

But in the end, the falsity of the idea that Gore had claimed to have invented the Internet mattered little to reporters all too eager to use it as a symbol of everything they didn't like about Gore. One network correspondent told *Rolling Stone*, "There just developed among a certain group of people covering Gore, particularly the print people, a real disdain for him. Everything was negative. They had a grudge against [Gore]. I don't know how else to put it."[99]

But for McCain, the rules are different. Where Kerry's expressions of patriotism only brought him suspicion, McCain's buy him respect. Where Dean's temper was overblown, McCain's is ignored. Where Gore's lifetime of public service was seen as the handiwork of an over-ambitious dork, McCain's elicits the press pack's reverence. The media love to hate, as the examples of recent elections show. But they also love to love, and in McCain they found someone they could love without reservation.

Chapter 3

Stuck with the Man

In 1999, E. J. Montini, a columnist for the *Arizona Republic*, had an interesting conversation with an out-of-town reporter. "The reporter from Atlanta wanted to know what the problem was between Arizona Sen. John McCain and the *Arizona Republic*," Montini recalled. "He said McCain's campaign people told him not to talk to reporters in Arizona, not if he wanted to get to know the real McCain."[1] The correspondent was also told by McCain's campaign "to speak with reporters in Washington, D.C." if he wanted to find out more about the senator—surely an odd recommendation. "Why would the McCain folks say that?" he asked Montini.

"Because they're smart," was the columnist's reply.

Montini knew of what he spoke. As a *Republic* writer, he had known John McCain since before he was a national figure, and had seen how Washington reporters came to view him far differently than their Arizona colleagues. As Montini wrote:

> Just about any member of the Washington press corps will be able to reel off three things about Sen. John McCain:
>
> 1. He's a war hero, having suffered through 5½ years in a North Vietnamese prison camp.
> 2. He's a maverick who's taken on his own political party in fights with Big Tobacco and campaign finance reform.
> 3. He's a straight-shooter, a lovable rogue who admits raising hell as a young man.

But having known the senator for much longer, Montini knew that such a depiction of McCain was the journalistic equivalent of an airbrushed pinup. "McCain is the most attractive political candidate in America, on the surface," Montini acknowledged. "And that's exactly where McCain's presidential campaign wants to keep it. On the surface."

A love affair took place aboard John McCain's Straight Talk Express during the 2000 presidential primaries, one truly unique in the history of American political journalism. And it has hardly waned in the years since. The media, usually known for their ravenous appetite for scandalous behavior, have conveniently left out the legendary tales of the senator's hair-trigger temper, his mean and vulgar sense of humor, and his questionable ties to shady characters. While reporters spill gallons of ink on McCain's admirable qualities, they have shoved to the side his unattractive traits, features of the McCain personality and record that he is no doubt all too happy to have the public overlook.

If one looks beneath the surface, one can find a treasure trove of stories and anecdotes about a McCain that would be unrecognizable to many Americans: short tempered, foul mouthed, bullying, and unscrupulous. Such accounts have been found mainly in Arizona media and less widely read sources. Those who have covered him the longest, the reporters of the senator's home state, have over the years done an admirable job of offering a full and complex portrait of the senator. For their efforts, these reporters have frequently been bullied by McCain—the stories of McCain's angry run-ins with reporters almost all concern those from Arizona—and largely ignored by the Washington press.

E. J. Montini says that Arizona reporters were once like the national media, smitten by the dynamic new lawmaker in the 1980s. But as with most love affairs, the passion cooled. "Over the years, though, contradictions surfaced," he wrote. "The campaign reformer cozied up to bigwigs he's supposed to regulate. The iconoclast trashed Big Tobacco but not Big Alcohol, financing campaigns with money from a beer distributorship owned by his wife's family."[2] As the *Arizona Republic* noted during his first presidential run, McCain "has romanced the national press while warring with Arizona reporters."[3]

McCain's character and record are worth discussing because for so long the press has portrayed McCain as a paragon of virtue, a man to whom the stereotype of politicians as calculated and venal simply does not apply. To grasp just how different his media image is, imagine for a moment if every politician were portrayed the way John McCain is. The focus would stay on their perceived greatest strengths, not their most glaring weaknesses. Reporters would retell the stories of candidates when they seemed at their best, not the moments when they were at their worst. Their "character" would be defined in the media by the noblest thing they had ever done, and the less flattering incidents would be pushed aside, to be dismissed if mentioned at all.

Whether such coverage would produce a more informed public better prepared to understand our nation's politics is debatable. What we do know is that the McCain the media have given us is all virtue and no vice—a veritable Washington superhero. The real John McCain, however, is all too human.

Senator Hothead

In its September 2006 issue, *Washingtonian* magazine published its biannual "Best and Worst of Congress" feature, a survey of Capitol Hill staffers on an array of irreverent categories, such as "Biggest Windbag" and "No Rocket Scientist." For the "Hottest Temper" category, the poll featured a perennial contender in the number two spot: Arizona's John McCain.[4] The second-place finish was hardly a surprise to readers of *Washingtonian*—it was the fifth time the Arizona senator had finished in the top three. Indeed, McCain's placement on the list wasn't news to any Washington insiders. Over the years, his temper has become legendary, a bit of Hill caricature on par with Robert Byrd's orotund speechifying or Ted Stevens's cantankerous rants. But for all of his blowups, John McCain has been blessedly unburdened with the reputation of being a hothead. A Gallup poll in August 2006 asked respondents to name what quality they disliked about John McCain. Only two percent cited his temper.[5]

In fact, *Washingtonian* published a story on it as early as 1997, titled "Senator Hothead," before McCain even began his ascent to iconic status. The article, however, was hardly a hatchet job. The lede prepares you for a portrait of the senator as an angry man: "John McCain bursts out of the cloakroom and onto the Senate floor. His face red, he rips off his glasses and gets ready to pound a table. Senator Hothead is mad. Again."[6] But instead of launching into a profile of an ill-tempered politician, the article paints a flattering picture. "In a Senate that still tries to present itself as a polite debating club, McCain stands out for his willingness to take on 'distinguished colleagues,'" reporter Harry Jaffe wrote. "McCain has fired back at some of the Senate's most treasured domains—campaign cash and pork-barrel spending—and damn the party affiliation." In other words, McCain isn't angry: he's passionate. When he blows his lid, it's only because he's standing up for his principles. Jaffe's interpretation would be repeated many times in subsequent years. Far from being a liability, McCain's temper becomes proof of his greatness, what makes him distinct from his bloodless and detached colleagues in the Senate. Where other politicians might be ridiculed as unhinged if they indulged in public outbursts (as Alaska's Stevens has been in the past), McCain's temper problem is viewed as proof of his passion for doing the right thing. And so it is that John McCain's short fuse is viewed not as a character flaw but a redemptive trait.

But not every reporter chooses to spin McCain's temper that way. While some national news outlets have in their archives a story or two about McCain's temper, the journalists who took a sustained look at the matter—and who concluded that it might be part of how his "character" should be understood—have been those who hail from the senator's own state. Pat Murphy, the former editor and publisher of the *Arizona Republic*, had this to say about John McCain in March 2000:

> If McCain were to become president, Americans would wake up to more than a commander-in-chief with a prickly temperament and a low boiling point. McCain is a man who

carries get-even grudges. He cannot endure criticism. He threatens. He controls by fear. He's consumed with self-importance. He shifts blame.[7]

Far from empty claims by an antagonistic journalist, Murphy's accusations are backed up by a long record of abusive behavior by the senator that has been minimized by the establishment media in his rise to superstardom. Senator Hothead, as the nickname suggests, can be mean and even vicious, something few Americans seem to know.

The state of Arizona is littered with stories of the senator giving full vent to his rage. One victim of his wrath was former Phoenix mayor Paul Johnson, a Democrat. At a meeting in Washington in 1992, Johnson got into a disagreement with McCain over a federal land swap deal. McCain, according to Johnson, said, "Start a tape recorder. It's best when you get a liar on tape." Johnson took exception to the remark, and before both men knew it, the two were nose-to-nose, ready to pounce on each other. "No blows were exchanged, but we were as close to being 14-year-old boys as we possibly could be," recalled Johnson. "Oh, gosh, you never dealt with a more brutal individual."[8] McCain, for his part, had a fuzzier recollection of that episode. Asked if he remembered calling Johnson a liar, McCain said, "No, I do not. I don't remember ever doing that."[9]

Johnson's judgment would seem unduly harsh were it not supported by similar accounts from other Arizona officials. In a 1993 incident, Kathy Dubs, a Republican member of the Phoenix City Council, questioned McCain's motives for supporting a proposed airport between Phoenix and Tucson. "He slammed his fist to the table and stood up and said this meeting is over," she recalled. "Then he pointed his finger at me and started calling me names.

His staff was pulling him back, trying to get him to sit down."[10] Judy Leiby, a former aide to onetime senator Dennis DeConcini (D-AZ), has also received the full brunt of the senator's vindictiveness. During her stint with DeConcini, Leiby made no secret of her displeasure with McCain and his staff's handling of Arizona veterans' issues. When DeConcini announced his retirement in 1994, Leiby received a surprise visit from McCain. Walking up to Leiby in a roomful of well-wishers, McCain told her, "I'm so glad you're going to be out of a job, and I'll see that you never work again." Asked later about the incident, McCain issued a familiar refrain. "No, I don't recall saying that, but it certainly didn't cause me any displeasure that she was out of a job," he told a reporter.[11]

Another high-profile dispute involved Grant Woods. Woods served as the state's attorney general from 1991 to 1999, and was on McCain's staff during his first congressional run. As a staffer, he helped to persuade his influential father, contractor Joe E. Woods, to throw his support behind the neophyte candidate. That support, according to Grant Woods, proved crucial to McCain's victory. In the succeeding years, Woods and McCain built a strong relationship that benefited both men's careers. But in 1994, their friendship began to fray. Woods began probing allegations that Governor Fife Symington's government had rigged the bidding for the state's cost-cutting program, Project SLIM. McCain, who was close with Symington, urged Woods to stop his investigations. Woods refused, to the loud displeasure of McCain, and the two men had a highly public falling out. "It appeared clear to me that the only way I could return to his good graces was to be a good boy, and I wasn't willing to be a good boy," said Woods in 1999.[12] (McCain and Woods have recently made up, in time for McCain's 2008 presidential run.)

McCain's close relationship with Symington also led to another rift. In 1994, Barbara Barrett, wife of Intel chief executive officer Craig Barrett, ran against the Arizona governor in the Republican primary. McCain pressured Barrett to withdraw from the race, an offer that Barrett refused. An enraged McCain threatened revenge. Barrett told the *New Republic*'s David Grann, "He asked my price to get me out of the race. Then, when I wouldn't succumb, he indicated he would use every ounce of his power to destroy me."[13] McCain admitted to the *Phoenix New Times* that he had threatened Barrett for running against Symington: "I told her there are consequences associated with causing other candidates to be defeated."[14] Later he characterized this incident slightly differently. "I may have spoken strongly with her," he said, "but I certainly never threatened political reprisals."[15] In other words, he "spoke strongly" with her and "told her there are consequences," but it wasn't a threat.

McCain also demanded that Maricopa County (Phoenix) Schools Superintendent Sandra Dowling drop her support for Barrett. When Dowling rejected McCain's demand, she said, McCain exploded and threatened to destroy her. "He told me that I was going to suffer the political wrath. . . . He was just flat-out mad," recalled Dowling.[16] The *Washington Post*, in a rare example of a major national newspaper going into detail about McCain's temper, said Dowling "had what eyewitnesses describe as a very angry confrontation with McCain, complete with curses and threats, in public view on the floor of the Republican state convention" in 1994.[17] When reminded of the incident, McCain simply laughed it off, alleging that it was Dowling, not he, who had lost composure.[18]

Though he was close to Fife Symington, McCain had a far less pleasant relationship with another Republican Arizona governor, Jane Hull. Upon hearing that Hull had given her endorsement to

George W. Bush in the 2000 Republican primaries, McCain expressed his disappointment in a civil fashion: "Although I was disappointed to learn of Jane Hull's decision to endorse Governor Bush, I am extremely confident that the statewide grass-roots organization of committed Arizonans that supported me in three consecutive elections to the U.S. Senate will bring me to victory once again."[19] But what McCain didn't mention was that Hull's endorsement may have come as a result of his shabby treatment of her. People close to both politicians have said that Hull had been the target of occasional flare-ups by McCain, including a demand that she fire her chief of staff. Speaking about McCain's temper to a *New York Times* reporter, Hull pretended to hold a phone several inches from her ear—enacting what it was like to be on the receiving end of a McCain outburst—and said, "We all have our faults, and it's something that John has to keep control of."[20] Grant Woods, speaking to the same *Times* reporter, accused the media of "gloss[ing] over big flaws" in McCain, particularly his anger. He added, "John McCain likes being the maverick but does not tolerate mavericks well. Governor Hull was not willing to be told how to do her job." Hull later said, "I would worry about who he surrounded himself with" if McCain became president. "If you interview people around here, you will find John's temper has exploded and pushed a lot of people away, just as it has a lot of senators."[21]

Other incidents have been chronicled and forgotten by the national media. A 1985 article in the *Atlantic Monthly* reported, "As freshman Joe Barton was walking down the center aisle of the House to cast a vote, he found himself in the middle of an angry crossfire of epithets between Democrat Marty Russo, of Illinois, and Republican John McCain, of Arizona. Seven-letter profanities escalated to twelve-letter ones and then to pushes and shoves before the two were separated."[22] During the confirmation hearings for defense secretary nominee John Tower, a close friend of McCain's, the Arizona senator was reported to have engaged in a shouting match in an elevator with Senator Carl Levin (D-MI), who opposed the nomination. "You should be ashamed of yourself," McCain was reported to have yelled. "So much for senatorial courtesy." The episode was reported in the "Washington Whispers" section of *U.S. News & World Report*, but was not picked up by any other outlets.[23] McCain yelled at another senator, Richard Shelby (R-AL), for voting against Tower, threatening that he would "pay for it."[24] In 1993, McCain antagonized Senator Ted Kennedy (D-MA), mocking the senator and telling him to "shut up." Kennedy responded in kind and told McCain to "act like a senator."[25] A right-wing Web site reported that a former senator who wished to remain anonymous recalled a Republican lunch meeting during which McCain called another senator "a shithead." The senator demanded an apology, to which McCain replied, "I apologize, but you're still a shithead."[26] During an argument with another senator, Chuck Grassley (R-IA), McCain said, "I thought your problem was that you don't listen. But that's not it at all. Your problem is that you're a fucking jerk."[27] At a 1999 GOP meeting, McCain erupted at Senator Pete Domenici (R-NM), the chairman of the Budget Committee. "Only an asshole would put together a budget like this," McCain was reported to have said. An offended Domenici replied with a restrained speech about how in all his years in the Senate, no one had ever called him that. Far from causing him to back down, Domenici's speech only made McCain push harder: "I wouldn't call you an asshole unless you really were an asshole." One Republican senator who witnessed the exchange told a reporter that he changed his mind about supporting McCain for president after the incident.

"I decided I didn't want this guy anywhere near a trigger," he said.[28] Another unnamed GOP senator, quoted by *Time*, suggested that McCain's temper had been genuinely detrimental to his effectiveness as a leader. "If he could just count to five sometimes, he would probably get a lot more done," said the lawmaker.[29]

But the powerful have not been his only targets. There have been instances of McCain blowing up at constituents as well. On election night in 1986, when he was first elected to the Senate, McCain flew into a rage at a campaign volunteer who had set up a lectern too high for the relatively short senator-elect, yelling and poking the young man in the chest. "Here this poor guy is thinking he has done a good job, and he gets a new butt ripped because McCain didn't look good on television," said Jon Hinz, who at the time was executive director of the Arizona GOP. "There were an awful lot of people in the room," Hinz recalled. "You'd have to stick cotton in your ears not to hear it. He was screaming at him, and he was red in the face."[30] In 1991, Dianne Smith, a sixty-three-year-old woman living in Phoenix, wrote the senator complaining about how McCain challenged Anita Hill's credibility before she testified in the hearings for Supreme Court nominee Clarence Thomas. Smith claimed that her letter, the first she had ever written to a public official, was neither rude nor impolite. Two weeks after sending it, she received a call from McCain. Clearly piqued by the letter, the senator "ranted on and on about what nerve I had to question his integrity. He was shouting, he was mad, I was absolutely taken aback," Smith recalled. When McCain was done berating her, he simply hung up.[31] In another incident, McCain snapped at a woman who approached him in an Arizona coffee shop during the Clinton impeachment to tell him his vote to convict was wrong. "Well, I've got four million other constituents. And they don't think lying under oath and obstructing justice is OK,"[32] McCain said none too civilly. That such episodes comprise a pattern seems obvious; that said pattern never becomes apparent in coverage of McCain tells us something about what reporters choose to print and what they ignore.

There may be no more frequent target of McCain's anger than reporters who fail to present him in a favorable light. Pat Murphy, for instance, was once good friends with John McCain. But the former editor and publisher of the *Arizona Republic* had a falling out with the senator over a 1989 story that was critical of McCain. The senator had told Murphy that he had planted tough questions with the Senate Interior Committee chairman to ambush the testimony of Arizona governor Rose Mofford, a Democrat, in favor of the Central Arizona Project, a water delivery system for urban areas. Murphy protested to McCain that the project had received bipartisan support for nearly half a century. To that McCain responded, "I'm duty bound to embarrass a Democrat whenever I can." When McCain's tactics were revealed in the pages of the *Republic*, McCain got on the telephone with Murphy and screamed, "I know you're out to get me!"[33] Murphy responded, "Now, John, for Christ's sake, act like a United States senator, not a goddamn child."[34] Murphy said that "war was declared" on him from that moment on, and he and McCain never spoke again. Years later, McCain admitted the dirty trick and apologized to Mofford, who was by then no longer in office.

Another reporter, Maureen Groppe, had a close encounter with an angry McCain. "I asked McCain if it would be difficult for him to win support for his finance reform bill when he was raising so much money from special interests," Groppe recalled. "He came up to me, put his nose really close, not quite touching, leaned his face into mine, and said, no."[35] Adrianne Flynn, an Arizona journalist, had a more vivid recollection of McCain losing it. "As I

pressed McCain for comment . . . he exploded," Flynn recounted
in an article for the *American Journalism Review.* "I remember his
face: scrunched as a Cabbage Patch doll and as red as a gale-
warning flag." When Flynn reported back to her superiors, she
found out that over-the-top responses from McCain were a regular occurrence. "Don't worry, my editor said, McCain does that a
lot. It'll blow over." But when Flynn transferred in 1995 to the
Arizona Republic, she learned differently. "My first day in the
bureau I learned that John McCain didn't talk to us. . . . Every
member of the newspaper's staff was persona non grata," Flynn
recalled. Flynn had to resort to tips from Washington reporters to
even know when and where the senator's press conferences would
be held.[36]

McCain's animus toward the newspaper continued through the
2000 primaries, when the McCain campaign even went so far as to
deny the newspaper's correspondent a seat on the campaign bus.
Instead, the reporter, Kris Mayes, was forced to rent a car and trail
the bus all around New Hampshire, even as reporters from
around the country by all accounts had a grand old time riding the
Straight Talk Express. It wasn't until Howard Kurtz, the *Washington Post*'s media critic, asked McCain about Mayes that the campaign finally relented and let her on, with less than a month to go
before the primary. Mayes said that the banishment was "absurd."
Compounding it, she pointed out, was the fact that "reporters [on
the bus] knew what was going on." Yet no one, outside of Kurtz,
reported McCain's exile of his hometown newspaper's correspondent from his campaign bus. Kurtz later commented, "Certainly
if a reporter from *USA Today* or the *Chicago Tribune* had been barred
from the bus, there would have been some sort of protest. Maybe it
says something about the self-importance of the national press."[37]

The subject of McCain's temper and vindictiveness has not been completely absent in national coverage of the senator. The stories are too numerous, the victims too willing to talk, for McCain's character deficiencies to remain completely unreported. Indeed, during McCain's first run for president, articles mentioning his temper did begin appearing in the mainstream media. Not surprisingly, it took an editorial from the *Arizona Republic* to draw others to the topic. In an October 1999 editorial titled "McCain's Temper Is Legitimate Issue," the *Republic* sought to make known nationally what was common knowledge to many Arizonans:

> If McCain is truly a serious contender for the presidency, it is time the rest of the nation learned about the John McCain we know in Arizona. There is much to admire. After all, we have supported McCain in his past runs for office. But the presidency is different. There is also reason to question whether McCain has the temperament, and the political approach and skills, we want in the next president of the United States.[38]

In response, McCain accused the newspaper of waging a personal vendetta against him in concert with the Bush campaign. Pam Johnson, executive editor of the *Republic* at the time, retorted that her paper's coverage was determined by the editors, not by rival political campaigns. "A lot of the admirable qualities of Sen. McCain have been widely reported nationally. A lot of the temperament issues have not," Johnson told the Associated Press.[39]

Following the editorial's publication, mentions of McCain's temper increased in the national media. In the month before the *Republic*'s editorial, there were thirty-six articles that mentioned McCain and his temper in the nation's newspapers, most of which only talked of it in passing. In the month after the editorial came out, there were more than two hundred and fifty stories that mentioned it. But a closer look at the coverage shows that even with the greater attention, the national media seemed to soft-pedal the concerns about McCain's temper. The *New York Times*, in a piece that appeared in its Sunday "Week in Review" section, pooh-poohed the concerns about McCain's short fuse. "As if presidential candidates don't already have enough tests of character to worry about—financial impropriety, drug use, adultery—now it seems they have to make nice as well," wrote Thomas Vinciguerra.[40] Addressing the allegations that McCain flew off the handle too easily, Vinciguerra mustered the rebuttal, "a hot temper seems almost a prerequisite for the Oval Office." In a New York *Daily News* editorial headlined "McCain Gets Mad? So What?" Lars-Erik Nelson wrote, "He has a temper, but he uses it for a purpose. The people on whom he vents his ire and the issue over which he works up a passion are both carefully chosen."[41] Such responses were typical from the national media in the wake of the *Republic*'s revelations. As *Editor & Publisher* noted following the publication of the editorial, "Much of the flak directed at the *Republic* is coming not from the senator and his supporters—but from the Washington reporters and other national media Big Foots."[42]

As a result of his temper, McCain has had to spend a lot of time making amends to the people he's offended. The letters of apology he has written over the years could fill volumes, according to observers. "There's a lot of those letters [of apology] floating around," said one of McCain's former aides.[43] "What Clinton is to empathy, McCain is to apology," *Slate*'s David Plotz noted.[44] In a number of cases, McCain has successfully mended fences with victims of his anger. And it should be noted that Washington is full of prominent figures, particularly members of Congress, who are known behind closed doors to be abusive toward their staffs. But here McCain is different. There appear to be no rumors of him berating those who work for him; rather, it is those who cross him—by supporting an opponent, standing in the way of something he wants to do, or simply disagreeing with him—who are on the receiving end of McCain's rage.

Despite countless stories concerning his volatile temper, McCain pleads innocent to the claims made against him. Responding to the charges of being a loose cannon, McCain said, "Do I insult anybody or fly off the handle or anything like that? No I don't"[45]— a contention that the *Arizona Republic* dismissed simply as "hogwash."[46] In another interview, he said, "I've never retaliated against anybody because that is not my view of the way you go through life."[47] In a 2006 interview with the Baltimore *Sun*, McCain was even more adamant:

> "Just because someone says it's there, you would have to provide some corroboration that it was. Because I do not lose my temper. I do not," he said. "Now, do I speak strongly? Do I feel frustrated from time to time? Of course. If I didn't, I don't think I would be doing my job. . . .
>
> "But for someone to say that McCain became just angry and yelled or even raised my voice or—it's just not true. It's simply not true. And so these rumors continue to circulate about—quote—temper. They're going to have to find some concrete examples of it, and they aren't there."[48]

Six months later, McCain would land yet again on the *Washingtonian*'s list for "Hottest Temper."

The Insensitive Type

Here's a joke:

> Why is Chelsea Clinton so ugly?
> Because Janet Reno is her father and Hillary Clinton is her
> mother.

That comic gem—which one would not be surprised to hear coming out of the mouth of Andrew Dice Clay, Ann Coulter, or Howard Stern—was delivered by John McCain at a Republican fund-raiser in June 1998, not long after Chelsea Clinton turned eighteen. McCain's delivery of the vicious two-liner was reported in some major newspapers. What was interesting, however, was that few of them reported the ugly joke in full. Among major news outlets, only the *Arizona Republic* and Associated Press reprinted the joke in full. The *Washington Post*, in a write-up buried in the personality section, said the quip "was too vicious to print." The *Los Angeles Times*, in its "Life & Style" section, also hinted at the joke, but did not reprint it for readers. The whitewashing was so blatant that Maureen Dowd wrote that the Arizona senator "is so revered by the press that his disgusting jape was largely nudged under the rug." (Her column, by the way, did not reprint the joke either.) Dowd also quoted a magazine editor who referred to the McCain-media love affair as "a return to the Kennedy era. He makes a gaffe, and we look the other way."[49]

And, indeed, it was a gaffe—just one that no one in the Washington media wanted to fixate on as they do with other politicians' gaffes. David Corn, Washington editor of the *Nation*, noted the hypocrisy of a press corps that refused to reprint a joke because of its viciousness but was more than willing to publish poorly sourced sexual innuendo involving Bill Clinton. "By censoring themselves," Corn wrote, "the *Post*, the *Times* and others helped McCain deflect flak and preserved his status as a Republican presidential contender." Corn added that "the joke revealed more than a mean streak in a man who would be president" and "exposed how the *Washington Post*, the *New York Times* and the *Los Angeles Times* play favorites when reporting the foibles of our leading politicians."[50]

John McCain's public career is dotted with incidents like this— a moment when the politician lets loose and delivers an impolitic line or crude jab that could get him in hot water, but doesn't because the press chooses not to cover it. His sailor's tongue has long been part of his appeal. It's part of the aura of "authenticity" that he has been able to create. Reporters know that when they're covering the senator, anything can happen.

Far from being careless, McCain is actually quite calculating in cultivating that image. "I get in trouble all the time and I will continue to get in trouble," McCain told an AP reporter. "I say what's on my mind to the frustration of my campaign people."[51] As with the joke about Chelsea Clinton, McCain's mean streak sometimes yields appalling quips that would normally land other politicians in hot water. During a trip to Boston in the 2000 primaries, McCain let loose with this chortler: "The nice thing about getting Alzheimer's is you get to hide your own Easter eggs."[52] On another occasion McCain referred to the Leisure World senior citizens' home as "Seizure World."[53] McCain realizes that while he may say something rude and offensive, the payoff—in the form of fawning coverage from a press corps that loves to reward "candor"—far outstrips the risks. Journalists reward him for it by calling him "refreshing" and "unscripted," while burying his offensive

quips and thoughtless remarks in the lower reaches of their tributes. As one senator complained to a reporter from *Newsweek*,
"He says things that would get us [negative] headlines, but he gets
a freebie."[54]

McCain has been insulated from the ravages of campaign coverage for other egregious missteps. During his many famous bull
sessions on the Straight Talk Express, McCain would blithely refer
to his Vietnamese captors as "gooks." McCain's use of the racial
slur was not mentioned by any reporter until September 1999,
when Roger Simon of *U.S. News & World Report* touched on the
reluctance of the campaign press corps to report it. "Strictly
speaking, one does not say 'gooks' anymore. It is simply not done.
But John McCain says 'gooks,' and who is going to tell him not
to?"[55] Simon wrote that the press had fallen so head over heels for
McCain that reporters had taken to telling him *not* to say incriminating things. One day, when McCain was riffing on politically
incorrect topics, Simon recounted, a reporter "just begged McCain
to shut up and protect himself." (Simon did not provide details of
McCain's allegedly offensive comments.) Try for a moment to
imagine a journalist telling Al Gore or John Kerry to be quiet lest
they say something juicy.

Simon's story about McCain's "gook" comment—which, its
revelation notwithstanding, was actually another in the endless
line of fawning stories about McCain—attracted some notice
here and there: *Slate*'s Jacob Weisberg mentioned the anecdote in a
piece a week later, and the *Washington Post*'s Howard Kurtz brought
it up in December. Weeks later, Robert Dreyfuss of the *Nation*
sought to revive the "gooks" gaffe with an article in the January 3,
2000, issue of the magazine. Still, no one else in the mainstream
media picked up what seemed an obviously newsworthy item: a

presidential candidate openly using a racial epithet. A search of all
news media in LexisNexis yields only six mentions of stories containing "John McCain" and "gooks" in the month following the
publication of Dreyfuss's article.

In the interim, however, the Asian-American community and
civil rights groups mobilized and circulated e-mails with the *Nation*
piece attached, complaining about McCain's irresponsible utter-
ance. The Asian American Journalists Association sent around
an e-mail criticizing McCain's "disparaging, racist remarks about
Vietnamese people."[56] Karen Narasaki, executive director of the
National Asian Pacific American Legal Consortium, issued a statement saying, "We're upset about the fact that he feels comfortable
using a racial slur while he's campaigning for president." Critics
also noted the media's complicity in keeping McCain's racist utter-
ances under wraps.[57]

In February, as grassroots anger grew over McCain's use of the
racial slur, the media finally began paying attention to the buzz
about the "gooks" story. February 2000 saw a steep increase in the
number of news stories about the "gooks" comment. There were
133 articles in papers around the country that mentioned both
McCain and "gooks." But, tellingly, the Washington press corps
stayed away. How many articles mentioning the subject appeared
in the *New York Times*? Two—one a more general story about
McCain's campaign that buried the "gooks" comment in the last
two paragraphs of a thirty-four-paragraph story,[58] and a sixty-
word brief buried on page fourteen.[59] For his part, McCain was
hardly contrite as the press began to pay attention. "I'll call, right
now, my interrogator that tortured me and my friends a gook,
OK, and you can quote me on that," he told reporters.[60] Not
backing down, he even added more fuel to the fire: "I will continue

to refer to them probably in language that might offend some people here. . . . I hated the gooks and will continue to hate them as long as I live."[61]

As with his use of the slur, McCain's non-apology received barely any attention in the establishment press. The only criticism of McCain's non-apology in the *New York Times* and the *Washington Post* came on the editorial pages—not in editorials, but in letters to the editor chiding them for ignoring McCain's insensitivity. "The lack of media and public reaction to Mr. McCain's statements and the failure to recognize this as an issue bearing on his fitness for the presidency is stunning," wrote *Times* reader Christopher Ho to the newspaper.[62] "Please explain how it is that Sen. John McCain can say, 'I hated the gooks and will continue to hate them as long as I live,' and be allowed to explain it away by referring to his storied tribulations as a POW," asked *Washington Post* reader Andrew S. Wolfe in his missive.[63] Even the Bush campaign noted the double standard. While their candidate was taking heat from the media for failing to speak out against the racist policies of Bob Jones University, a South Carolina university that did not allow interracial dating, McCain was getting off scot-free for his explicitly racist epithet. As columnist Stephen Chapman noted, "What is most amazing here is that the ['gooks' comment] was almost completely ignored by the national news media. By now, in contrast, most voters probably think George W. Bush is the founder and president of Bob Jones University."[64] In the end, despite the Washington media's inattention, the brewing discontent among Asian-American groups and in the Vietnamese-American community forced McCain to back down. A barely repentant McCain retreated from his earlier position and issued a reluctant apology: "I will continue to condemn those who unfairly mistreated us. But out of respect to a great number of people whom I hold in very high regard, I will no longer use the term that has caused such discomfort."[65]

The apology put the issue to rest, but the episode revealed the curious dynamic between McCain and the national media. Simply put, the Washington press corps downplayed the "gooks" story. It took enormous grassroots pressure for the media to even bring the story up at all. While there are no recent examples from presidential campaigns that precisely parallel this incident (Joseph Biden got a good deal of immediate attention for saying in 2007 that Barack Obama was "the first mainstream African-American who is articulate and bright and clean," but he was not viewed as a leading candidate at the time), it is safe to say that had any other contending candidate used a racially derogatory term so publicly, it might well have spelled the end of that person's candidacy. In the 2006 midterm elections, Virginia senator George Allen (R) found himself at the center of a media firestorm when he used the word "macaca" to refer to an Indian-American campaign worker from opponent Jim Webb's camp. As some commentators pointed out, "macaca" is a derogatory word meaning "monkey" that originated in North Africa, and Allen's mother was born and raised in Tunisia, a former French colony in North Africa. The videotaped incident became a national story immediately, prompting extensive coverage in the *Washington Post* (which has many readers in Virginia) and wall-to-wall coverage on the cable shows. By some accounts, the gaffe effectively torpedoed the Allen campaign. Allen would go on to lose the election, despite having been touted as not just a shoo-in for reelection but a potential U.S. presidential candidate as well.

Making off-color jokes or using insensitive language shouldn't disqualify John McCain from the presidency; it would be naïve to think that our leaders, even the best of them, have not made an offensive remark or two in their lives. But the media's look-the-other-way policy when it comes to McCain is remarkable. Again, imagine another politician in the same context—say, Al Gore making a vicious joke about the Bush twins' physical appearance, or John Kerry letting slip the word "gook" and justifying it with his Vietnam duty. The press, not to mention the right-wing media machine, would have a field day. When George Allen uttered "macaca," they did—and that was for a racial epithet that few people had heard of before. But what would be a campaign killer for other politicians is just another outrageous zinger from John McCain. "He delivers these stupid lines all the time," said Weisberg. "The typical response from journalists is either to not report it or to congratulate him for being so blunt instead of treating it as a gaffe."[66] NPR's Mara Liasson explained, "They're not considered gaffes because reporters have a context . . . if you have two hours to talk to John McCain and he mentions—he calls the Vietnamese 'gooks,' but you know that this isn't a bigot talking."[67] In other words, because of the relationship McCain has established with reporters, he gets the benefit of the doubt when other candidates wouldn't.

There are two John McCains visible in the media. One is a straight-talking maverick, a lovable rogue, a man of charm, wit, and honesty. The other is all those things at times, but at other times is a vindictive, petty man who lashes out with uncontrolled rage at anyone who questions or opposes him. The first John McCain is the one known to the Washington-based national media—and as a result, known to most voters. The second John

McCain is known to political insiders in Washington, as well as to members of the Arizona press corps, who have had the longest and most sustained contact with the senator. E. J. Montini of the *Arizona Republic* likened the differing perspectives on McCain to the difference between a mistress and a wife. The former is infatuated and lovestruck, aware of only the lover's best qualities. The latter, however, is "stuck with the man."[68]

Chapter 4

Not-So-Straight Talk

*Senator John McCain, Republican, Arizona, is a **maverick**, a conservative, a **Vietnam POW** who survived five bitter years in prison in Hanoi, and he wants to be president of the United States. He also **wants to clean up the money mess in Washington**. McCain says that a torrent of campaign cash has turned the nation's capital into a cesspool of corruption. A couple of months ago, before all the recent headlines about fund-raising scandals and White House videotapes, we started following McCain around, knowing **that he was going to challenge the Senate and his own political party to clean up their act**. Well, it's been a tough week for this **gutsy rebel**, as his own party leader did him in on the floor of the Senate.*

—*60 Minutes*, October 12, 1997

This introduction to a 1997 *60 Minutes* profile of John McCain managed to pack nearly all the key McCain tropes into a few sentences. Veteran newsman Mike Wallace, who reported the story, later said, "I'm thinking I may quit my job if he gets the nomination . . . I'm impressed by his independence, by his willingness to take on the tough ones. By his honesty about himself. As I look at the current crop, there's something authentic about this man."[1]

This story, and many like it from the period before he made his first run for president, focused on McCain's campaign finance reform effort and how it made him the establishment-bucking reformer reporters were growing to love. The Myth of McCain says that out of the ashes of the Keating Five scandal, a reformer was born, one who became a sworn enemy of that perennial Washington villain, "special interests." Perhaps no other senator in the last decade or two has become as synonymous with a legislative crusade as McCain has with campaign finance reform. It is inarguable that a considerable part of his mystique stems from his apparent willingness to fight a long, thankless battle against K Street, facing off against entrenched interests and his own party in his quest. Depicted by the media as a reformer looking to oust the money changers from the temple, McCain finally saw passage of his signature bill, known popularly as McCain-Feingold, in 2001 (it was signed into law in 2002), helped along by a rash of corporate scandals that gave his long-languishing cause sudden urgency.

Even if we grant that the passage of McCain-Feingold (officially called the Bipartisan Campaign Reform Act) was a significant success given the amount of time it took and the opposition it received from most Republicans, the magnitude of the accomplishment has been inflated beyond all reasonable proportion. On the strength of this one legislative success, McCain has become the beneficiary of a drastically revisionist take on his career by the media, canonized as the reformer untouched by the sleaze of money-driven politics. But the record tells a different story. For throughout McCain's political life, one can see the hallmarks of the hustling politico—the reliance on powerful lobbyists, the close ties with industries in his regulatory purview, the specter of conflict of interest.

McCain has always asserted that the Keating Five experience changed his outlook toward the influence of money in politics.

But in a March 2006 article in *Legal Times*—hardly a publication widely read by the general populace—readers could glimpse a side of McCain that they rarely see. In a story titled "Straight Talk Express Travels Down K Street," reporter Joe Crea expressed bemusement at the utopian musings of pundits who believed that a McCain victory in 2000 would have broken the lobbyists' hold on Washington:

> Toss the lobbyists from the temple? Someone must have overlooked the fact that McCain's 2000 campaign manager was lobbyist Richard Davis, who would go on to register a bevy of telecom clients—all of whom had business before the Commerce, Science and Transportation Committee, which McCain chaired until late 2004. During the 2000 race Big Telecom money poured into McCain's campaign. Overall, the Center for Responsive Politics estimates that businesses with interests before the Commerce Committee contributed more than $500,000 to McCain's presidential bid.[2]

Unfortunately, such realistic assessments of McCain are few and far between. One rare instance came in 2000 on the Comedy Central program *The Daily Show*, when correspondent Steve Carell sat down with McCain aboard the Straight Talk Express in New Hampshire. "Senator," Carell asked, "how do you reconcile the fact that you are one of the most vocal critics of pork-barrel politics, and yet while you were chairman of the Commerce Committee, that committee set a record for unauthorized appropriations?" McCain looked stunned, and after an uncomfortable silence, Carell blurted out, "I'm just kidding! I don't even know what that means!" Everyone laughed.[3]

For someone who inveighs against the influence of money on

politics, however, McCain has a pretty impressive war chest himself. In the 2006 election cycle, Straight Talk America, McCain's leadership political action committee, brought in just under $8 million, a take that included donations from individuals at Southwest Airlines, JP Morgan Chase, Akin Gump Strauss Hauer & Feld (one of the top Washington law/lobbying firms), the DCI Group (another prominent lobbying firm), American Defense International, and Microsoft's government affairs office, to name a few.[4]

For his 1998 Senate run, McCain took $562,000 in contributions from the communications industry[5] (he raised $4.4 million for that race—more than ten times as much as his opponent, Ed Ranger). Before his next reelection campaign, he received $900,000 more, lagging only five senators among telecom beneficiaries.[6] He also amassed $341,000 from airlines, railroads, and other transportation companies. Between 1993 and 2000, McCain collected $685,929 from media corporations, the most of any sitting member of Congress.[7] What do these companies have in common? They all have interests before the Senate Commerce Committee, which McCain chaired at the time. The Center for Responsive Politics reported that eight of the top ten contributors to his 2000 campaign were executives in those industries. One top fundraiser, Sol Trujillo, was chairman of US West, which stood to benefit from McCain-sponsored legislation that would permit Baby Bells to offer high-speed Internet access.[8]

The communications industry has been a significant backer throughout McCain's career. And McCain has used his position of authority on the Commerce Committee to bestow favors upon his generous donors. In 1999, McCain sponsored a bill that allowed satellite-TV operators to transmit local network signals. (The previous federal law on satellite transmission of local signals was scheduled to lapse that spring; networks opposed such transmissions from satellite operators, deeming it tantamount to piracy.) One week after the bill cleared McCain's committee, Charlie Ergen, founder of EchoStar Communications, a satellite television concern, threw a fund-raiser at his Denver home for the Arizona Republican, raising $47,000. The bill eventually passed Congress. A couple of years later, McCain was also one of the leading voices against Rupert Murdoch's acquisition of DirecTV. DirecTV is, of course, the biggest competitor to EchoStar's Dish Network.

Another telecommunications company that benefited from McCain's support is BellSouth. In 1998, McCain wrote to the Federal Communications Commission on behalf of the company, which was seeking permission to expand into the long-distance business in Louisiana. BellSouth had given McCain's campaign $60,000 over the years up to that point, and had allowed the senator to use the company jet. Another telecom, Ameritech, was the beneficiary of McCain's political sponsorship. Ameritech was in the middle of a merger with SBC Communications, a deal that had to pass muster with regulators first. In an April 1999 letter to the FCC, McCain chastised the agency for "applying a different, and much stricter, burden of proof in this merger proceeding than the commission has applied in evaluating other mergers."[9] He wrote another letter a month later criticizing the commission for letting a staff member attack the merger. The FCC eventually approved the merger. Ameritech, for its part, has been energetically pro-McCain. The company and its employees had given McCain's 2000 campaign $12,000 and its chief executive officer, Richard C. Notebaert, had served as a cohost of a McCain fundraiser that brought in $88,000.[10]

Another industry with which McCain has cultivated good relations is the gambling industry. According to the Center for Responsive Politics, gambling interests donated more than $100,000 to McCain between 1993 and 2000. Over the years, McCain has cast votes that benefited the industry, from legislation paving the way for gambling "cruises to nowhere," to granting casinos tax exemptions for the free meals they give to workers, to striking down legislation that would have halted the expansion of gambling onto Indian reservations.[11] For the most part, the press has ignored McCain's ties to these industries.[12]

And then there is the alcohol industry. When he was elected to Congress, McCain vowed that he would recuse himself on all votes relating to the alcohol industry. After all, the industry gave McCain's father-in-law and wife their fortune, the fortune that helped jump-start his political career. A *Phoenix New Times* study in 2000 found that McCain had in fact recused himself from some two dozen alcohol-related bills that had come up for a vote. However, the *New Times* found that McCain exerted his influence in other, less obvious ways. As Commerce Committee chairman, McCain was able to kill regulatory legislation on alcohol simply by sitting on bills. For instance, in 1997, momentum was gathering for Senate hearings on broadcast advertising by liquor companies. Seagram's decision in the summer of 1996 to air ads on network TV—violating a longtime voluntary ban by the distilled-spirits industry—was seen as a potentially dangerous precedent. As alcohol and beverage companies and legislators girded for a fight that might have led to tighter regulations on alcohol advertising, hard liquor, beer, and wine industry political contributions doubled during that session of Congress. By February 1997, however, the Commerce Committee announced it would not delve into the beer and wine industry's role in alcohol advertising. The *New Times*'s Amy Silverman, analyzing the committee's decision, reported, "Clearly, the pressure the beer and wine lobby brought to bear on

many members of Congress had something to do with the decision, but observers also wonder about the coincidental timing of
John McCain's ascent to the chairmanship of the Senate Commerce Committee."[13]

One might think that McCain's donors and his actions on the
Commerce Committee would be the subject of substantial
scrutiny given his high profile and national ambitions. But this has
not been the case. Nor has McCain's choice of associates over the
years been given much attention—and there might be a story or
two there, for reporters who care to look. Charles Keating was, of
course, one of McCain's closest sponsors, an ethically tainted figure whom McCain gladly had in his corner while his usefulness
lasted. Then there was Darrow "Duke" Tully, the former publisher of the *Arizona Republic* and one of McCain's earliest sponsors and close friends (Tully is the godfather of one of McCain's
daughters). McCain would probably never have had a political
career without Tully, who was a member of the "Phoenix 40," an
informal group of wealthy and powerful businessmen, including
those who controlled many of the major media outlets in the city.
As the *New York Times* described it, the group was "the closest
thing to a political machine in Phoenix, and anointment by the
Phoenix 40 almost invariably translated into victory at the polls."
In 1982, the group chose to back McCain instead of other Republicans with lengthier Arizona ties who had been waiting to run for
an open congressional seat.[14] One of the state's most powerful
men, Tully was forced to resign in 1985 when it was revealed that
he had fabricated his military record. There was also Governor
Fife Symington, long a close McCain ally. In 1997, Symington was
forced to resign after being convicted on multiple fraud charges
involving millions of dollars of loans secured from lenders. (The
conviction was later reversed when the judge threw off an inco-

herent juror; Symington was eventually granted a presidential pardon.)

Then there are the people whom McCain chooses to work for him. Many McCain associates are enmeshed within Washington's corporate-political establishment in ways that would seem to call into question McCain's bona fides as an opponent of "business as usual." In fact, there is a revolving door between McCain's inner circle and the lobbying industry he claims to despise. McCain's 2000 campaign manager was Rick Davis, a former White House aide to Ronald Reagan. Davis is a name partner in the lobbying firm Davis, Manafort & Freedman, Inc. The firm had four clients around the time of McCain's primary run: GTECH Corporation (a gambling concern), phone company SBC, Comsat (a government owned satellite company), and Fruit of the Loom, Inc. Comsat and SBC had major mergers pending before the FCC in 1999, both of which were approved.[15] In 2007, the McCain campaign confirmed that Tom Loeffler, a former Republican congressman, head of the lobbying firm that bears his name (the Loeffler Group) and "Super Ranger" for President Bush (meaning he personally raised over $500,000), would become McCain's "consigliere" for his presidential race.[16]

That isn't to say that a typical presidential campaign won't count corporate lobbyists among its staff and supporters. But McCain is supposed to be different. And in preparation for his 2008 presidential run, McCain went even further, seemingly hiring as many former advisers to George W. Bush as he could, including some who do not bring to mind words like "honesty" and "character." Terry Nelson, for instance, was forced to testify about his involvement in two separate GOP corruption scandals, one involving Tom DeLay's alleged money laundering, and the other involving a Republican scheme to jam the telephone lines of the

New Hampshire Democratic Party to sabotage their get-out-the-vote efforts on election day 2002. In the former, Nelson was an unindicted coconspirator[17] who was allegedly involved in a scheme to move money between the Republican National Committee and the Texas Republican Party in violation of Texas election laws. In the latter, Nelson was the boss of James Tobin, the Republican Party operative who was convicted for his role in the phone-jamming scheme. In 2006 Nelson ran the Republican Party's independent expenditure arm, which was responsible for the infamous "Harold, call me!" ad in which a young white woman squeals that she met African-American Tennessee Democratic Senate candidate Harold Ford "at the Playboy party" and implores him to call her, presumably for sex.

In March 2006, McCain made Nelson a "senior adviser" to his Straight Talk America PAC, then announced in December that Nelson would manage his 2008 presidential campaign. (Appearing on Don Imus's radio show, McCain said of Nelson and the ad, "He did not design it, but he made a mistake in approving it. He recognized that mistake, and he resigned from that group." This was false: Nelson publicly defended the ad, and there is no evidence that he resigned from the RNC over it. Even Wal-Mart, which had hired Nelson to help it spruce up its image, cut its ties with the consultant.) Nelson would leave the campaign in July 2007 in a shake-up following poor fund-raising performance; he was replaced by Rick Davis.

The hiring of Bush campaign veterans was hardly the only overture McCain made to the Republican establishment. At the end of 2006, conservative columnist Bob Novak wrote of an event that had just taken place: "Thirty invited corporate representatives and other lobbyists gathered at the Phoenix Park Hotel on Capitol Hill Tuesday to hear two senior mainstream Republican senators pitch the 2008 presidential campaign of Senator John McCain. They were selling him to establishment Republicans as the establishment's candidate."[18] In fact, McCain was as aggressive in courting Bush donors as he was in scooping up Bush staffers. When the *Arizona Republic* examined the contribution reports from McCain's Straight Talk America PAC in December 2006, they found that in addition to signing up a number of Bush's "Pioneers" and "Rangers" (major donors who had raised over $100,000 or $200,000, respectively) to raise money for him, McCain had raised $1.4 million from former Bush donors. At this time—before he officially announced his campaign—seven out of ten of those Bush donors were giving to McCain for the first time.[19]

These efforts to become the "establishment" candidate— historically a sure path to the Republican presidential nomination— would turn out to be a major misstep for McCain, undermining his maverick image even as it failed in its immediate goal of winning over that establishment. But it wouldn't have been too shocking for anyone who had followed McCain's career closely and noticed that for a champion of political reform, McCain has a lot of friends and associates who are lobbyists or corporate bigwigs. For instance, Sol Trujillo, the CEO of US West, a Colorado-based telecom that was up to that point McCain's biggest career patron, was national finance cochair for McCain's 2000 campaign. Working alongside Trujillo as national finance cochair was Herb Allison, the former president and chief operating officer of Merrill Lynch & Co., Inc.—another generous McCain donor. Another one of his campaign's primary fund-raisers was Timothy McKone, a senior lobbyist for Davis, Manafort & Freedman. McKone was actually the point person for the SBC-Ameritech merger. In February 2000, an analysis of Federal Election Commission records by the Center for Responsive Politics showed that McCain had accepted rides on corporate jets thirty-five times during the campaign.[20] McCain also has close ties to a number of high-profile "superlobbyists" such as Kenneth Duberstein, Vin Weber, and Fred Zeidman, who signed on to the McCain presidential campaign in 2007 as his liaison to the Jewish community. (News reports did not indicate whether Zeidman objected when McCain hired longtime Republican bankroller Fred Malek in April 2007 to be his campaign finance cochair. As an aide in the Nixon White House, Malek was assigned to count the number of Jews in the Bureau of Labor Statistics, which Nixon believed contained a Jewish "cabal" seeking to undermine his presidency.)

One could look at the list of McCain's lobbyist connections, or his corporate fund-raising, or his campaign filled with many of the people who put and kept George W. Bush in office, and say it's just how the system works. The same might be said of anyone immersed in the Washington establishment for a quarter of a century. But McCain's message has always been that he may be in the system, but he is not of it. Speaking in 2000, a veteran Washington lobbyist was blunt about McCain: "He's hustling the same guys the rest of 'em are. No more, no less."[21]

Get on the Express

What makes a straight talker? For one, he says what's on his mind, regardless of the political consequences. In the public imagination, it also extends beyond talk and into the realm of action: straight talk means taking a definitive and unshakable stand on an issue. The typical politician avoids taking a stand unless he really has to; a straight talker takes a stand even when it hurts him. This definition certainly fits John McCain as the media have presented

him to the public. As *U.S. News & World Report* contributing editor
and CBS News national political correspondent Gloria Borger
asserted in a 2006 column, "No one would accuse McCain of
equivocating on anything."[22] No one in the press, anyway.

In truth, McCain has been just as guilty as other politicians of
attempting to be all things to all people. McCain's public statements are dotted with fuzzy, platitudinous answers in response to
tough questions. Far too frequently, most of the media have given
credit to McCain for saying something emphatically, ignoring the
disconnect between substance and rhetoric. On the campaign trail
in 1999, for example, when McCain was asked whether he supported California's controversial Proposition 209, a ballot initiative striking down affirmative action quotas, he said this: "I
support the concept, [but] I thought it was unfortunate we had to
go to a ballot initiative to do so." He elaborated, "In Arizona,
we've been able to sit down with our Hispanic citizens and talk
about how we can help increase opportunities, help with greater
education, with better admissions into our major universities, and
we've made great success and we didn't have to go to a ballot initiative to achieve these goals."[23] Can anyone parse exactly what
McCain thinks of affirmative action from that answer? In sum-
ming up his views for 2000 primary voters, the *National Journal*
wrote, "McCain supports affirmative action, although he's somewhat inconsistent on the subject. He opposes quotas, but has
denounced initiatives that attempt to eliminate quotas or racial
preferences."[24] "Inconsistent" is one word for such a confusing
tangle of beliefs.

Hints that McCain's views on policy might not be particularly
deep are often ignored if they can be mistaken for "straight talk"
by reporters. Commenting on the horrific sectarian violence in
Iraq, McCain said in 2006, "One of the things I would do if I were

president would be to sit the Shiites and the Sunnis down and say, 'Stop the bullshit.'" That line came at a 2006 event where he presented himself "as the straight-talking political independent."[25] The idea that all the Iraqis needed was a swift kick in the pants might have marked McCain as a deeply unserious thinker when it came to foreign affairs and national security—had anyone bothered to notice.

One of McCain's more high-profile wafflings during the 2000 campaign came in South Carolina. During that stretch of the Republican primary, both McCain and George W. Bush were asked about their views on the hotly contested issue of whether the Confederate flag should fly over the statehouse there. Depending on how you look at it, the issue presented either a test of character or a political catch-22 (anger conservative South Carolinians or anger lots of other people elsewhere whom you'll need in the general election). When asked about his thoughts on the Confederate flag by CBS's Bob Schieffer, McCain had responded, "The Confederate flag is offensive in many, many ways, as we all know. It's a symbol of racism and slavery."[26] However, just days later, McCain gave the answer that many South Carolina conservatives wanted to hear: "Personally, I see the flag as a symbol of heritage."[27] McCain said that the decision over whether the flag should fly over the state's capitol should be left to South Carolina's voters, a position no different from George W. Bush's—and one universally seen as a way of dodging the issue.

After the primaries, when the need to curry favor with conservatives had passed, McCain sang a different tune again. Angling himself back toward the center, he admitted that he had pandered and that his statements on leaving the issue of the flag up to the voters had been motivated by politics rather than principle, even calling it "an act of political cowardice."[28] Was he condemned for speaking out of both sides of his mouth? Not exactly. "Senator John McCain displayed political courage—belatedly, but power-fully—in apologizing for his failure to protest South Carolina's official use of the Confederate battle flag," said a *New York Times* editorial.[29] "The real value of Mr. McCain's extraordinary remarks would be if they shamed all politicians who pander and straddle," opined the *Washington Post*.[30] Yet the mistake has never been held against him because he expressed regret. By adding the coda of the apology to the story, what had been a blatant act of pandering ceases to be an incident demonstrating that McCain is like other politicians and instead becomes just the opposite. These days, when one encounters discussion of the 2000 South Carolina pri-mary, one is more likely to find mentions of the Bush campaign's tactics against McCain there than McCain's selling out of prin-ciple for the sake of the southern vote.

McCain's refusal to reveal his true feelings on the Confederate flag wasn't his only dalliance with retrograde views in the South. One of McCain's key South Carolina advisers in 2000 was Richard Quinn. As the *Nation* reported, "Before the primary, Quinn orga-nized a rally of 6,000 people in support of flying the Confederate flag over the statehouse. Quinn dressed up McCain volunteers in Confederate Army uniforms as they passed fliers to the demon-strators assuring them that McCain supported the Confederate flag."[31] In addition to being a political consultant, Quinn is the former editor of the neo-Confederate magazine *Southern Partisan*. He also once wrote an article speaking out against naming a holi-day after Martin Luther King Jr., calling such an act "vitriolic and profane," and characterizing King's legacy as "lead[ing] his people into a perpetual dependence on the welfare state."[32] In 1989, he wrote a piece hailing another national political figure as a "maver-ick": David Duke.[33] Several news articles in 2006 noted that

Quinn is working with McCain once again on his 2008 campaign as the senator's top adviser in South Carolina—but none mentioned Quinn's controversial background.[34]

Despite McCain's lack of clarity on this and other issues, the Arizona senator retains his reputation for "straight talk," a trope repeated again and again in stories about McCain, hundreds of times a year. Interviewers regularly precede their questions to McCain with requests that he deliver his signature "straight talk." Katie Couric asked him, "Why don't you just give us a little straight talk, Senator, and tell us when you'll announce you'll be running for president?"[35] One McCain appearance on *Today* featured an on-screen title, "Straight Talk from John McCain."[36] And as McCain began his second run for the presidency, the frequency with which the term was repeated increased rapidly. Even as some began to question whether he was being true to his "straight talk" history, the idea was still firmly wedded to McCain; when a reporter mentions "straight talk," there's no doubt which politician is being discussed.

Standing Tall, or Not

For a few fateful days in September 2006, John McCain held the media and the country in thrall. The senator so often described as a "maverick" was in a familiar place—the center of attention—facing off against the Bush administration, this time over the issue of the treatment of detainees suspected of involvement in terrorism. As the administration campaigned for the passage of a bill giving it authority to question detainees using "alternative interrogation methods" and eliminating their habeas corpus rights, the Republican senator from Arizona stepped into the spotlight and challenged the legislation. McCain said that the issue was not

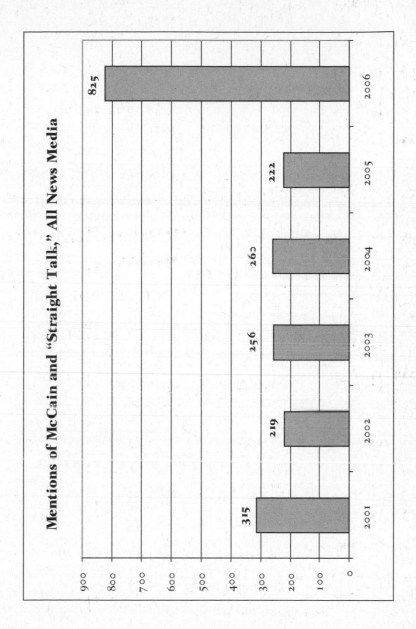

Mentions of McCain and "Straight Talk," All News Media

Year	Mentions
2001	315
2002	219
2003	256
2004	262
2005	222
2006	825

about who the terrorists are but who we as Americans are. He argued against the bill's proposed redefinition of the Geneva Conventions of 1949, a change that the administration believed would give interrogators greater latitude to engage in abusive practices while still staying within the confines of the law. Such a change, McCain claimed, was not just an unacceptable transgression of American values, but counterproductive as well. "Weakening the Geneva protections is not only unnecessary, but would set an example to other countries, with less respect for basic human rights, that they could issue their own legislative 'reinterpretations,'" said McCain.[37] Indeed, the Bush bill was truly revolutionary, breaking with two centuries of American ideals about justice, law, and the limits of government power by codifying the abusive treatment of detainees and the elimination of their due process rights.

In John McCain, critics of the administration had seemingly found their champion, and the media framed the issue as a showdown between McCain and the administration. McCain was the central actor in the drama, quoted in story after story, sought out for interviews, brought onto the Sunday news shows to explain why he was opposing the president for whom he had campaigned so enthusiastically two years before. Forcing the administration to sit down at the negotiating table and hammer out a compromise bill, McCain and fellow dissenter senators Lindsey Graham (R-SC) and John Warner (R-VA) were praised for staging a "Republican rebellion"[38] and "courageously push[ing] a competing bill."[39] The press portrayed McCain as taking a valiant stand, fighting for his principles despite the political harm it might do him. "McCain is working hard to woo the conservative voters who form the core of Bush's political base, and he may risk alienating those voters by straying from Bush's national security policies," wrote the *Los Angeles Times*.[40]

McCain's crusade, it was said, transcended politics; it was personal. "You speak with a little authority on this as a former POW yourself in Vietnam," CNN's Wolf Blitzer told the senator.[41] McCain, wrote the *San Diego Union-Tribune*, "brings unimpeachable moral authority to the debate over the legal and moral limits on detainee interrogations. As a prisoner of war in North Vietnam for five and a half years, McCain was severely tortured."[42] The *Christian Science Monitor* agreed: "Senator McCain, a former prisoner of war in North Vietnam, knows torture firsthand and brings moral authority to the issue."[43]

After days of tense talks, a new bill emerged. The compromise on the Military Commissions Act of 2006 was hailed as a win for McCain and his allies. The *New York Times* foregrounded the fact that Bush dropped his demand to redefine the Geneva Conventions, dubbing it a victory for McCain.[44] The *Los Angeles Times* was more explicit, proclaiming in a front-page headline, "Bush Bows to Senators on Detainees."[45] ABC News's Martha Raddatz stuck to the same theme, reporting, "The White House blinked on this."[46] With that, another episode in the legend of McCain entered posterity. Courageously risking the anger of his fellow Republicans, he had demonstrated his independence, stood firm on principle, and won.

Or did he? As legal experts and human rights advocates pored over the bill in the days following its passage, they came to an ominous realization: the "compromise" legislation was hardly a compromise at all. In passing the bill, Congress had effectively given the executive branch untrammeled powers that violated the very notion of checks and balances. The bill granted the president the power to designate and detain indefinitely any noncitizen he decides is an "illegal enemy combatant" with no judicial oversight. The bill failed to address the question of American citizens, whom the Bush administration has long claimed also can be declared enemy combatants and detained indefinitely. Any suspects detained under the act would be stripped of their due process rights to challenge their designation as enemy combatants or the legality of their detention. The legislation also prohibited the courts from reviewing any aspect of the detainee program, except for the verdicts of the specially created military tribunals—which, because the bill imposed no time limits on the government, could be delayed as long as the president wants. Moreover, the bill immunized any government officials from prosecution for prior violations of detainee abuse laws. As for the Geneva Conventions McCain had said he was defending, the bill actually gave the president "the authority for the United States to interpret the meaning and application of the Geneva Conventions," essentially giving him the power to ignore them if he wishes.

In short, the bill gave the White House almost everything it wanted; it was McCain who blinked. As Dan Bartlett, counselor to the White House, said at the time, "We proposed a more direct approach to bringing clarification [to the detainee program]. This one is more of the scenic route, but it gets us there."[47] The administration gave ground on only two areas: allowing suspects to see evidence the jury sees at the tribunals, except for classified details, and disallowing evidence obtained by torture. But the president reserved the right to define torture however he wishes, meaning all manner of abusive practices could continue. Though McCain had persuasively summoned a tradition of American principle in his initial objections, he evidently came around to the administration's outlook, one that found it acceptable for the president, on nothing but his say-so, to lock people up for life and subject them to "alternative methods" of interrogation, all beyond the purview of the courts.

"It only takes 30 seconds or so to see that the Senators have capitulated entirely, that the U.S. will hereafter violate the Geneva Conventions," concluded law professor Marty Lederman, writing on the legal blog *Balkinization*.[48] Robert Kuttner, in an op-ed for the *Boston Globe*, noted that the resulting bill "looked uncannily like the original administration bill."[49] Commentators, so extravagant in their praise of McCain during the negotiations, were likewise critical of the finished product once they had the chance to examine it. The *New York Times* editorial page denounced it as a "tyrannical law that will be ranked with the low points in American democracy, our generation's version of the Alien and Sedition Acts."[50] Law professor Bruce Ackerman, writing in the *Los Angeles Times*, called the bill a "dangerous compromise" that "would haunt all of us on the morning after the next terrorist attack."[51]

Yet in the week or so between the announcement of the "compromise" and the more thorough analyses of the final product, McCain seemed to disappear from the story. Though he had received reams of praise while the negotiations were going on, once the bill's details were revealed, hardly anyone in the news media held McCain accountable for his role in its creation. His image as a maverick senator standing up for principle and bucking the president remained intact. The condemnations of the final bill assailed Bush for its distasteful provisions, but not McCain for the role he had played in its passage. But the story was not yet over. "After approving the bill last Friday," the *Boston Globe* wrote, "Bush issued a 'signing statement,' an official document in which a president lays out his interpretation of a new law declaring that he will view the interrogation limits in the context of his broader powers to protect national security. This means Bush believes he can waive the restrictions, the White House and legal specialists said." In other words, Bush simply proclaimed that he would ignore even the toothless compromise whenever he pleased. McCain's only response was to issue a statement with fellow Republican John Warner saying they expected the president to follow the law.

Over his twenty-five-year career in Congress, McCain has established himself as the exemplar of bipartisanship, independence, and moderation in the nation's capital. A closer inspection, however, reveals that the image is newsprint-thin. The debate over the torture legislation may perhaps be seen as little more than a footnote in the long political career of John McCain. But it casts in sharp relief nearly everything important about McCain, both the politician and the media-created persona. In the story told by the media, McCain took a principled position, bravely standing up to his own party and its leader. The press noted again and again how his courageous stance grew from his experience as a prisoner of war in Vietnam. He was, it was said, showing yet again what a "maverick" he was, someone unconstrained by partisan interests or political calculation, doing what was right because that's just the kind of guy he is.

But there is another, more plausible version of this story. In this version, McCain's move was hardly courageous, since he was taking a position clearly popular with the electorate.[52] McCain made a very public show of opposing the Bush administration— then politely caved. He did this knowing the media would shower him with praise when it looked like he was taking a brave stance, and then turn away and ignore his capitulation on the principles he claimed to hold. In short, what could have been a story of opportunism followed by failure and defeat became yet one more chapter in the Myth of McCain, the story of a maverick, a man of ideals, the last best hope for a better politics.

. . .

In the media, at least, John McCain seems to have a monopoly on "straight talk." He's the one who'll tell it like it is, who'll tell us what we don't want to hear, who'll give us the truth unadorned by slick sound bites and carefully crafted spin. Above all, he's different from the rest of the blow-dried, relentlessly preening and calculating politicians who stalk the halls of Congress.

Yet despite this image of John McCain as a unique politician, what one sees upon close examination is that in many ways he is no different from others who seek and hold high office. He has been ambitious and opportunistic, he has received financial help from those who seek the favors of the government, many of his friends have turned out to be unsavory characters, he has condemned "special interests" while maintaining close relationships with corporate lobbyists, and he has cultivated a reputation for high ethics while employing ruthless and ethically challenged political operatives. Could each of these charges be leveled at many other politicians? Absolutely. But that is precisely the point.

Chapter 5

With Moderates Like These . . .

For a few weeks in 2004, Democrats clung to the hope that a Republican would be their party's vice presidential candidate. The end of the Democratic primary season in March inaugurated a period of fevered speculation about whom John Kerry, the Democratic nominee, would choose as his running mate. While several Democratic up-and-comers were bandied about as possibilities, the most tantalizing option was a Senate veteran, and a Republican to boot: John McCain. McCain seemed intrigued by the notion initially. In a March 10 morning show interview, McCain admitted that he would "entertain" the idea of being the Democratic vice presidential candidate if asked, a comment that set off an eruption of Beltway hype. By that evening, however, he sought to put out the brush fire he'd started. McCain, said his chief of staff emphatically, "will not be a candidate for vice president in 2004."[1]

But in the heady climate of a presidential campaign, conjecture frequently trumps reality. And so it was that the next couple of months saw the idea of a Kerry-McCain dream ticket gain currency. Although no formal offers were made (or rejected), Washington was abuzz with rumors that Kerry was putting on the full-court press to recruit his Senate colleague. Big-name Democrats, even those with vice presidential aspirations, talked up the possibility of a Kerry-McCain ticket. Dick Gephardt, fresh off losing in the Democratic primaries, said that McCain is "someone a lot of Democrats could get interested in."[2] Florida senator Bill Nelson said a Kerry-McCain combo "feels right."[3] Delaware senator Joe Biden urged McCain to be "a more loyal American than . . . a loyal Republican" and consider the Democratic VP slot.[4]

The press was just as captivated by the scenario. Week after week, stories and columns surfaced about the possibility of a Kerry-McCain ticket. David Ignatius of the *Washington Post* said McCain could not say no simply because the country's future depended on his acceptance.[5] But McCain could not have been clearer about his decision even as speculation ran wild. "Could I also finally say, I am not a candidate for vice president of the United States in 2004 and I will not leave the Republican Party, end of story?" said McCain in late March.[6] "I will not leave the Republican Party," McCain told Tim Russert in mid-April.[7] "I have totally ruled it out," he reiterated to the *New York Times* in May.[8] Finally, in June, a *Times* headline seemed to signal the media's surrender to reality: "McCain Is Said to Tell Kerry He Won't Join."[9]

It was not the last time the question of John McCain becoming a Democrat would be raised. In early 2007, the Capitol Hill newspaper the *Hill* reported that in 2001, McCain strategist John Weaver had approached prominent Democrats about the possibility of McCain switching parties. Tom Daschle, who was at the time the Democratic leader in the Senate, said he and McCain had had discussions about the possibility. McCain and his aides asserted that he never seriously considered a party switch.[10]

Were it not for the widespread belief that John McCain is something other than a reliable conservative, the idea that he might become part of a Democratic presidential ticket—or become a Democrat at all—would have been dismissed out of hand by all concerned as simply ridiculous. After all, just two decades earlier, the Arizona Republican had entered Congress trumpeting his allegiance to Barry Goldwater and Ronald Reagan. Yet in 2004, McCain found himself courted by liberals, who were desperate to have him rescue the Democratic Party from its electoral doldrums. In the end they failed—and the result was one more round of glowing media coverage for John McCain.

"This Man Is Not a Republican"

In the 1980s, John McCain was hardly a national figure, nor one known for being anything other than a conservative Republican. During the '90s, however, McCain began to develop a reputation for party apostasy for his positions on campaign finance reform and tobacco regulation. But such highly public breaks with the party were, in fact, aberrations.

On the campaign trail in 1999 and 2000, however, the "maverick" conservative became something else in the eyes of the reporters who covered him. Now they were describing him not just as someone who enjoyed rebelling against his party, but as an *actual ideological moderate*. A headline in the January 31, 2000, issue of the *New Republic* summed up the euphoric delusion inspired by McCain's campaign: "This Man Is Not a Republican."[11] The profile of McCain, published in the heat of the primary season, made the case that the Republican senator had, in the course of his run, morphed into a moderate Democrat. Two years later, the magazine—and the piece's author, Jonathan Chait—published another article on the same theme, subtitled "Why John McCain Is the Democrats' Best Hope."[12]

Yet up until his 2000 run for the White House, McCain had been regularly described in the press as a "staunch conservative." Even the conservative *Washington Times* described McCain in 1995 as "a staunch conservative and a decorated Vietnam War veteran and former POW."[13] He was able to change that image not by altering his positions on fundamental issues, but by planning a few showy acts of bipartisanship that delighted Democrats, peeved Republicans, and served to distort his overall record. Anyone watching coverage of McCain over the ensuing years would come to believe that some sort of ideological transformation had taken place, to the point where McCain was no longer a conservative at all and had become not just a moderate but the most prominent moderate in Washington. "McCain has emerged as the leader of moderates in both parties," raved one profile.[14] One prominent Democrat called him "the leader of the loyal opposition."[15]

Writers invoked Theodore Roosevelt as the model for McCain, a comparison that the senator encouraged. "His political philosophy places him closer to Theodore Roosevelt than to his other idols, Barry Goldwater and Ronald Reagan," wrote John Judis in the *New Republic*.[16] "John McCain could reinvigorate the party should he succeed Bush, just as the equally magnetic Teddy Roosevelt did when he took office following McKinley's assassination in 1901," wrote James Traub in the *New York Times Magazine*.[17]

"Essentially, McCain is a progressive. He's a modern version of Teddy Roosevelt," *Newsweek* quoted one conservative activist saying.[18] Less frequently mentioned were two other heroes of McCain's political life, Reagan and Goldwater.

The uncritical categorization of the Arizona senator as a moderate (the *New York Times*'s William Safire once even called him a "hard-line moderate"[19]) continues to this day. Despite recent high-profile flip-flops to the conservative side on issues such as the Bush tax cuts and intelligent design, McCain still enjoys more support among Democrats and liberals than nearly any other Republican politician. "Psst . . . he's not really a conservative," argued Jacob Weisberg, the editor of *Slate*, in 2006.[20] No less a progressive stalwart than Ralph Nader penned a tribute to McCain in the May 8, 2006, issue of *Time*, in a feature titled "Leaders & Revolutionaries."[21] That piece appeared just two weeks after *Time* named McCain one of America's ten best senators, dubbing him "The Mainstreamer."[22] Despite the questions raised about his efforts to reach out to the right wing, the Arizona senator is still seen as the epitome of sensible, pragmatic centrism in American politics.

To be sure, McCain's inflated reputation as a moderate did not come out of thin air. After Bush took office in 2001, McCain pursued a few legislative goals that were anathema to the hard-right orthodoxy of the Republican Party. McCain collaborated with John Edwards and Ted Kennedy on a patients' bill of rights. He worked with Charles Schumer on a generic prescription drug bill. With Joe Lieberman, he pushed to close the gun show loophole and reduce greenhouse gas emissions in compliance with the Kyoto Protocol. McCain also sponsored, with John Kerry, legislation raising auto emissions standards.

It is tempting to look at the examples of McCain cosponsoring a policy change with a Democrat or criticizing a conservative activist and conclude, well, maybe he really *is* a maverick and a moderate, and all the glowing coverage that built and sustains that image is perfectly justified. No one would argue that McCain is nothing more than a lockstep GOP loyalist, or that he has never reached across the aisle. He certainly has—but so have innumerable other senators. The vast majority of those who represent an entire state (unlike House members, many of whom represent ideologically homogeneous districts) see it in their interest to have some bipartisan credentials to which they can point when it comes time for reelection. Even the most ideologically consistent senators will find bills on which they can affix their name along with members of the other party.

A look at voting patterns in the Senate hardly shows that all Republicans always vote with Republicans and all Democrats always vote with Democrats. Instead, while there are a few who come close, most vote against their party at least occasionally. In fact, it would be more accurate to say that *every* senator votes against his or her party some of the time. *Congressional Quarterly* tracks what it calls "party unity" votes, those on which a majority of Republicans vote against a majority of Democrats. The results show that there is practically no such thing as a senator who is loyal to his or her party 100 percent of the time. In the 108th Congress, for instance, Republicans had party unity scores ranging from Lincoln Chafee's 69.5 (290 votes with the GOP out of 417) up to Craig Thomas's 99.5 (412 out of 414). There was one senator that year who got a score of 100: John Kerry, who because he was campaigning for president voted on only 138 party unity votes, less than half of those that actually took place. It was the first time in forty years that a senator achieved a score of 100. McCain's score for that Congress was 84.3.[23]

In short, if asked, every senator could point to at least a few votes on which they disagreed with their party or joined with those who were usually their opponents for a particular effort. Paul Wellstone and Jesse Helms, probably the most progressive and conservative members of the Senate, respectively, when they served, cosponsored bills together on China's human rights violations. Hillary Clinton has joined with Republicans on a variety of issues, but no one calls her a maverick.

To appreciate how much political mileage McCain has gotten out of his few well-chosen breaks with other Republicans, consider the contrast with Clinton. As long as she has been in public life, Clinton has held many positions that are ordinarily associated with Republicans, supporting the death penalty, numerous free-trade agreements, and high defense spending, to name a few. She was also a strong and early supporter of the Iraq war (though she became a critic as the war dragged on). Yet these positions are not only not taken as evidence that she is in fact a centrist, they are used as evidence of insincere political calculation. She has often been characterized as *moving* to the center in preparation for a presidential run, even when her position on the issue in question has remained unchanged.

For instance, when Clinton said that pro-choice and pro-life people could find common ground by trying to reduce the number of abortions through increased access to birth control, it was called "an attempt to move to the center as she contemplates a presidential run in 2008."[24] Chris Matthews asked whether "she'll have a problem reconciling her current move to the center with her past image as sort of a Madame Defarge of the left."[25] Paul Gigot of the *Wall Street Journal* described her alleged changes in position as a "makeover and move to the center that she's now attempting. So, I mean, she's a shrewd politician, and that's why she's attempting it."[26] NPR's Mara Liasson practically saw Clinton spinning in circles: "She is doing what her husband did. Which was not so much move to the center or the right, but figure out a way to bridge the left-wing base of the Democratic Party. And move to the center at the same time."[27] Yet she was not changing her position on anything. For her entire time in public life, Clinton has been pro-choice and has supported access to birth control. Pointing out that such access would reduce the number of abortions, something anti-abortion forces ought to favor, cannot fairly be described as a shift in any direction.

For Clinton, long-held positions, like a hawkish approach to military affairs, are taken as evidence of a shift. And the prevailing assumption is that when she breaks with some in her party (or even when she sticks with her party) it is for crass political purposes and not an outgrowth of genuine conviction. Yet for McCain it is just the opposite. Whether his occasional breaks with the GOP are the product of pure conviction, pure calculation, or something in between, they are seldom if ever characterized as being motivated by politics. The idea that he could be adopting a position insincerely contradicts the image in the press's mind of who John McCain is. So the question of whether he is doing so on a particular occasion is barely ever asked. His sincerity is simply assumed, the context in which his actions must be understood

Finding the Popular Position

So how did McCain manage to create the impression that he is not just a maverick but a moderate as well? He was able to find a few high-profile issues on which to dissent from his party and draw maximum attention to his supposedly heroic acts of independence. Once his "maverick" status was established, it became self-perpetuating: when others might be ignored for the instances in which they vote against their party, every case in which McCain does so is given unusual attention and taken as yet more proof that he is a moderate maverick.

The very word "maverick" implies not only independence but a willingness to take risks. But it is critical to understand the common thread running through McCain's high-profile breaks with the GOP: *in nearly every case, McCain took a position that was overwhelmingly popular with the public.* It was hardly a risk for a politician with national ambitions to embrace campaign finance reform or an effort to regulate tobacco,[28] despite the displeasure it may have caused within the GOP caucus. The other issues on which he has broken with some or all Republicans—global warming, the gun show loophole—were also cases in which the prevailing Republican position was widely unpopular. However sincere he was in the positions he took, the result in every case was a double victory for McCain: he could enhance his image as a moderate and a maverick, and do so with no risk to his national ambitions, since he was taking the popular position.

If we consider cases in which others took real risks to stand on principle, the contrast is striking. For instance, Russell Feingold was the only member of the Senate to vote against the USA PATRIOT Act. Coming as soon as it did after September 11, this vote held real political danger, as the act was at the time overwhelmingly supported by the public (though they may have had little idea what it actually contained). Nebraska Republican senator Chuck Hagel, representing one of the most conservative states in the country, began to criticize the Iraq war long before it became fashionable to do so. None of McCain's breaks with his party remotely resemble Feingold's action, or even Hagel's. To the contrary, he has chosen areas in which the GOP is clearly on the wrong side of public opinion to make his "maverick" stands.

No issue had a greater role in cementing his image as a reformer in journalists' minds than campaign finance reform. For many reporters obsessed with the behind-the-scenes process of politics, the issue represented all that was appealing about John McCain. Never mind that the bill McCain was advocating was far less expansive than its supporters touted, or that McCain's fund-raising was—and remains—as prodigious as almost any other senator's. According to the Center for Responsive Politics, which tracks campaign finance, McCain raised over $70 million between 1986 and 2006. In his 2004 reelection campaign, he spent $4.6 million despite facing only token opposition from a candidate who spent less than $13,000.

Look at immigration, another issue on which McCain would like us to believe he is taking a "maverick" stance (when asked whether his courting of the far right in advance of the 2008 election threatened his "maverick" credentials, he said, "I don't think that my position on immigration is exactly pleasing to the far right base"[29]). Here again, we see him finding the most popular position to take when he opposes not even his entire party, but just a piece of it. The bill he introduced in 2005 with Edward Kennedy (D-MA) contained provisions on border security and enforcement, but most notably would have established a guest-worker program and created a lengthy path to citizenship for illegal immigrants. Though some in the Republican Party were vehemently opposed to such a path to citizenship, the public at large supported it overwhelmingly. A *Los Angeles Times*/Bloomberg poll found that 67 percent of Americans were in favor of such a proposal and only 18 percent opposed it.[30] A Gallup poll offering respondents a choice between deporting all illegal immigrants, allowing them to stay but only for a limited time, or offering them a path to citizenship found 16 percent favoring deportation, 17 percent favoring limited stays, and 66 percent favoring a path to citizenship.[31] In other words, though there might have been some loud voices in his party favoring more extreme solutions on immigration, McCain once again got praise as a maverick for favoring the most popular solution.

In all these cases, something important happens in the media when McCain opposes his party. When an ordinary senator crosses party lines, he or she will join members of the other party and perhaps have occasional opportunities to be quoted or interviewed on the issue in question. But the larger story will remain one of partisan conflict, albeit with a senator here or there breaking party unity. When McCain crosses party lines, on the other hand, the story itself changes: it then becomes a story about John McCain and his rebellion. If McCain joins Democrats on an issue like campaign finance reform or tobacco regulation, then he becomes the spokesperson the media turn to for that side of the issue. He will be invited on Sunday talk shows to debate a Republican on the other side. He will be quoted in every major article on the topic. Gradually, Democrats will almost disappear from the issue entirely, no matter how much they may have worked on it, as the media present the entire conflict as one not between the two parties with a few defectors on each side, but between the Republican Party and John McCain. This is the most important reason that McCain is perceived to be much more of a maverick and an independent than the moderate Republicans like Olympia Snowe or Susan Collins who actually break with the GOP far more often.

The hostility that McCain's high-profile defections have engendered from conservatives only served to convince reporters further that he really is a centrist and a maverick. Campaign finance reform has long been a bane of the corporate elite that props up the Republican Party, and McCain's independence on the issue predictably led to harsh attacks from some forces on the right. His break with the party on the Bush tax cuts was likewise met with disdain among hard-line conservatives. Stephen Moore, head of the conservative Club for Growth, said in 2001, "He used to be a pretty reliable fiscal conservative. Clearly there has been a full metamorphosis. . . . His rationale [for opposing the tax-cut bill] looked like it was written by Tom Daschle, with all of its talk of class warfare."[32] In Arizona, McCain's controversial positions even gave rise to a fringe recall movement. "The last straw was when he voted against the tax cut," said Marcia Regan, head of the Recall John McCain Committee.[33] The attacks on McCain from the right only enhance his image as a rebel going his own way.

A Moderate or a Conservative?

So just how moderate is John McCain? Amid all the admiring coverage of his alleged revolts against his party, few people have really stopped to scrutinize the claims that have been made about his ideological transformation. Much of the coverage of McCain in the popular press during the first congressional session after his 2000 campaign focused on the issues on which he diverged from party orthodoxy. Considering that such breaks constituted only a fraction of his activity as a U.S. senator—every year, McCain casts hundreds of votes, most with other Republicans—it's fair to say that coverage of McCain suffered from a certain tendentiousness. The press cropped the big picture, obscuring the details that would have contradicted the portrait it was painting.

Take abortion. The man who would have been John Kerry's

running mate is, and has always been, a reliable opponent of abortion rights. Over the years, McCain has voted for cutting federal funding of family planning clinics that counseled pregnant women on abortion. He has supported a ban on late-term abortion and pushed for parental notification before minors can have an abortion. He has consistently received zero ratings from NARAL Pro-Choice America and Planned Parenthood. In 2000, hard-line social conservative Gary Bauer actually endorsed McCain over Bush. When asked why, Bauer said it was because when he asked both candidates whether they would appoint pro-life candidates to the Supreme Court, Bush said he would have no litmus test, while McCain simply said yes.[34] In 2006, McCain announced that he would have signed an anti-abortion bill recently passed in South Dakota, which banned all abortions except when necessary to save a woman's life. The blatantly unconstitutional law was passed in a bid to challenge *Roe v. Wade* (South Dakota voters later overturned the measure in a ballot initiative). Given these facts—and despite some of the rhetorical gyrations McCain has gone through on the issue—it appears that McCain's true position on abortion is farther to the right than Bush's. (It is worth noting that Bush has managed to run two presidential campaigns and serve two terms in the White House without ever giving a yes-or-no answer to the question of whether he would like to see *Roe* overturned.)

Over the years, McCain has also expressed a range of views that would make any Democrat and plenty of moderates blanch. He has opposed extending the assault weapons ban, federal hate crimes legislation, the establishment of the International Criminal Court, the Comprehensive Nuclear-Test-Ban Treaty, pro-labor legislation, ergonomics rules, lawsuits against gun manufacturers, and benefits for gay partners. He has supported privatizing Social

Security, conservative judicial appointments, the teaching of intelligent design in public schools, tax cuts for the wealthy, and the posting of the Ten Commandments in public schools. And that is before we even get to McCain's views on national security.

A Hawk's Hawk

On defense and foreign policy, it is not easy to imagine how a senator could be more conservative than McCain. Though we may now think of George W. Bush as the very model of bellicosity in foreign affairs, when they faced off in the 2000 Republican primaries, it was McCain who took the more aggressive position. As he said in one of their debates,

> I would also . . . revise our policies concerning these rogue states: Iraq, Libya, North Korea—those countries that continue to try to acquire weapons of mass destruction and the means to deliver them. . . . I'd institute a policy that I call "rogue state rollback." I would arm, train, equip, both from without and from within, forces that would eventually overthrow the governments and install free and democratically elected governments. As long as Saddam Hussein is in power, I am convinced that he will pose a threat to our security.[35]

The monomania of removing Saddam Hussein had been coursing through neoconservative circles throughout the 1990s. The attacks on 9/11 gave the neocons the opening they needed to put their radical plan into effect—a project to which McCain gladly signed on. McCain had supported a now-famous 1998 letter to Clinton from the Project for a New American Century, calling for the U.S. to overthrow Saddam Hussein, by force if need be and without "a misguided insistence on unanimity in the U.N. Security Council."[36] *Weekly Standard* editor William Kristol, the chairman of PNAC and perhaps the best known of the neoconservatives (not to mention a staunch supporter of McCain's), has said of McCain that "his views on foreign policy are neoconservative: American strength, but also American principles; for nation-building, as well as for removing dictators."[37] Foreign policy for his 2008 campaign is coordinated by Randy Scheunemann, one of the key figures in PNAC.[38] Scheunemann also headed the Committee for the Liberation of Iraq, an organization established to advocate for an invasion of Iraq (the CLI ceased operations, as Scheunemann's bio on the PNAC Web site states, when "its mission was completed in 2003").

Before the war began, McCain pushed the administration's talking points as relentlessly as anyone. Saddam Hussein, McCain argued in September 2002, "is intent on constructing weapons of mass destruction," adding, "particularly a nuclear weapon."[39] That same month, he said, "I believe that the success will be fairly easy."[40] In January of 2003, he said, "We will win this conflict. We will win it easily."[41] Just one week before the invasion, Chris Matthews asked McCain on MSNBC's *Hardball*, "Do you believe that the people of Iraq or at least a large number of them will treat us as liberators?" McCain replied, "Absolutely. Absolutely."[42] Yet four years later, when the war had become seemingly intractable, McCain rewrote his own history and that of the Congress. "When I voted to support this war, I knew it was probably going to be long and hard and tough," McCain said, "and those that voted for it and thought that somehow it was going to be some kind of an easy task, then I'm sorry they were mistaken. Maybe they didn't know what they were voting for."[43]

Those disturbed by the Right's recent demonization of dissent should note that when McCain was asked on the day the Iraq war started whether protests against the war would cease, he responded, "Well, I hope so. Because, you know, there comes a time for debate and discussion and protests, and then there comes a time when we should rally behind the president and the troops when we go into a conflict.

"Look, it's not possible to only support the troops and not their mission," McCain went on. "I mean, that's just a contradiction."[44] One could argue that this is little more than an un-American slander against the millions of citizens who consider the men and women serving in the military to be brave and honorable, but also believe that the government that puts them in harm's way can sometimes be wrong. One might also note that McCain said this at a time when the war was supported by two-thirds of the American public, but when public opinion turned against the war, he was careful not to repeat the charge that those who opposed the war were failing to support the troops.

It was not the only time McCain would assert that dissent was out of bounds. When North Korea attempted a nuclear test in October of 2006, a debate quickly ensued about whether the Bush administration—which had been in office for six years—was more responsible for the heightened threat than the Clinton administration. "I think this is the wrong time for us to be engaging in finger pointing," McCain said, "when in this crucial time, we need the world and Americans united."[45] Yet the day before, McCain said, "The fact is that it is a failure of the Clinton administration policies . . . that have caused us to be in the situation we're in today."[46] But now, McCain said, it was "not appropriate at this moment to be critical of President Bush."[47]

As more and more Americans did become critical of President Bush over Iraq, McCain's advisers unsurprisingly portrayed his

support for the Iraq war as a reflection of his principled straight
talk unmoored from any crass political considerations. "McCain is
a straight shooter," said his political adviser John Weaver in April
2006. "It is stay-the-course, no matter what. And if it dooms
McCain, so be it."[48] Supposedly liberal columnist Richard Cohen
agreed. "Anyone who knows McCain appreciates that his call for
more troops in Iraq is not, at bottom, part of any political strategy," Cohen wrote. "McCain is a thoroughly admirable man. Like
any other politician, he will punt when he has to, but he is fundamentally honest, with sound political values."[49] Anne Kornblut
of the *New York Times* agreed. "Senator McCain is proving that
he is nothing if not an independent-minded maverick on this,"
she said.[50]

Yet even as support for the war diminished, it remained popular among the voters who would be deciding the 2008 GOP primaries. And "stay the course" was something McCain repeated
often—until it became politically unfashionable. "We've got to
stay the course," he told ABC News in October 2004.[51] "I think a
year from now," he said in December 2005, "we will have made a
fair amount of progress if we stay the course."[52] By September
2006, he was growing uncomfortable with the language, but not
the policy, telling CBS News that he thought Bush had "laid out
recently a pretty cogent argument why we must quote—I hate to
use the phrase—'stay the course.'"[53] By mid-October—by sheer
coincidence, just as the administration was pulling away from
its use of the phrase and stressing how flexible and nimble their
Iraq policy would continue to be—a West Virginia newspaper
reported that at an event for a local candidate, "The senior senator
from Arizona said he was not an advocate for a 'stay the course'
policy in Iraq."[54] While Bush was ridiculed for making this same
semantic two-step, no one asserted that McCain was flip-flopping.

If nothing else, Bush and McCain are joined by the fact that both men's fates are tied inextricably to the outcome of the Iraq war. In 2004, McCain made more campaign appearances for the president than he did for his own reelection run in Arizona. "I thought it was a lot more important for him to be reelected than for me to be reelected," McCain said at the time, which could sound like admirable selflessness if you didn't know that polls showed McCain with a lead of over fifty points over his opponent, so he had no need to campaign for his own reelection. Later, he attested, "Campaigning with George W. Bush was one of the proudest moments of my life."[55]

For all the credit McCain is given as an authoritative voice on foreign affairs, few reporters note that it is not just Iraq that binds him and Bush together. The truth is that, like Bush, McCain is an unabashed hawk, a neoconservative in all but name, secure in his belief that only U.S. power can preside over a volatile and dangerous world. This perspective has guided American foreign policy since January 2001, and the results have been less than encouraging.

The Right Stuff

We don't have to go by subjective impressions to determine McCain's conservative bona fides. Every year, interest groups rate lawmakers on how they vote on particular issues. Sure enough, conservative groups give John McCain high grades for his performance on their behalf in the U.S. Senate. For instance, in 2006 the American Conservative Union gave him an 65 percent rating, meaning that John McCain voted with the interests of the group 65 percent of the time. Throughout his career, McCain has ranked consistently high on the group's year-end ratings. Compare McCain's 2006 ACU ratings with those of other senators who are described in the press as moderate Republicans. Susan Collins and Olympia Snowe of Maine each scored 48 percent and 36 percent respectively; Lincoln Chafee of Rhode Island came in even lower at 24 percent. On the other hand, Ted Stevens of Alaska, understood by reporters to be a solid conservative, had a rating of 64 percent—the same as McCain (the typical Democrat gets a rating under 10 from the ACU; only one, Nebraska's Ben Nelson, has a lifetime rating over 50).

Other advocacy group ratings attest to McCain's conservative bona fides. Concerned Women for America, a group dedicated to bringing "Biblical principles into all levels of public policy,"[56] rated McCain highly, grading him a perfect 100 percent for the 2006 congressional session. Another powerful right-wing group, the Christian Coalition of America, rated McCain at 83 percent in their most recent scorecard.[57] Americans for Tax Reform, the organization headed by conservative stalwart Grover Norquist, no fan of McCain, nonetheless gave the senator a 80 in their most recent scorecard, a testament to his fealty to his ideological roots.

Liberal groups, in turn, are unsurprisingly sour on McCain's legislative record. Americans for Democratic Action, which has been rating lawmakers for decades, gave him a "liberal quotient" rating of 15 percent in 2006. His lifetime average from the group is a mere 9 percent.

So much for McCain being a moderate. But what about his alleged willingness to buck the GOP and go his own way? The truth is that McCain's breaks from his party are actually few and far between. *Congressional Quarterly*'s "party unity" ratings, which track the frequency with which lawmakers vote with other members of their party, show that McCain has been a reliable GOP foot soldier throughout his career.

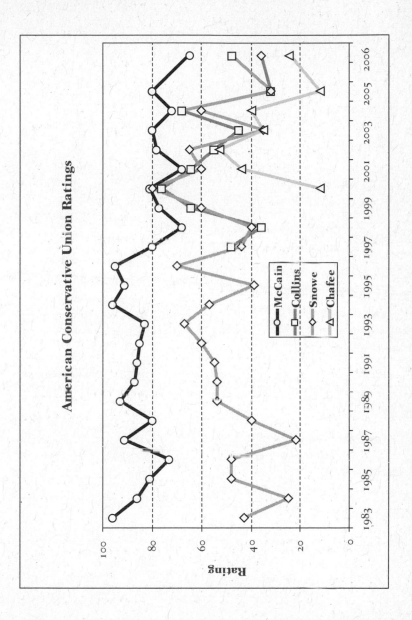

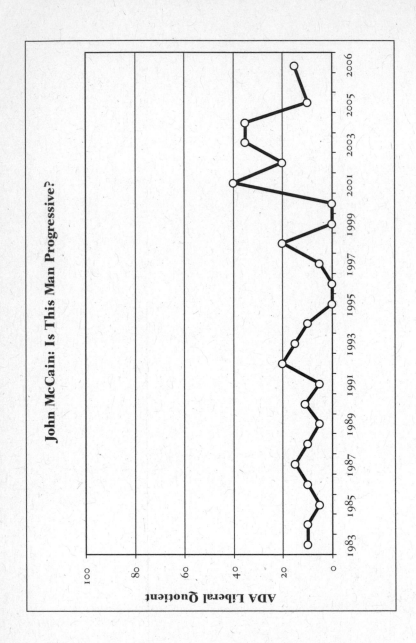

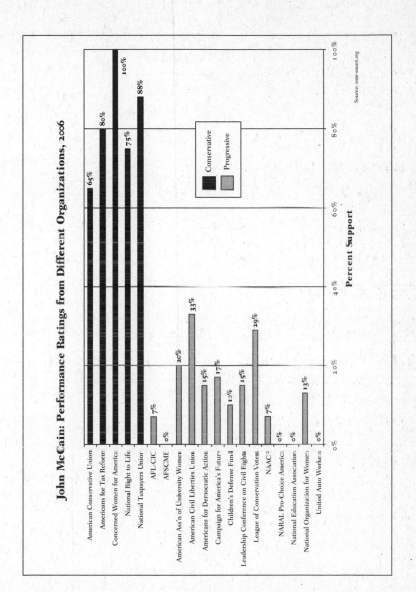

John McCain: Performance Ratings from Different Organizations, 2006

Percent Support

Source: vote-smart.org

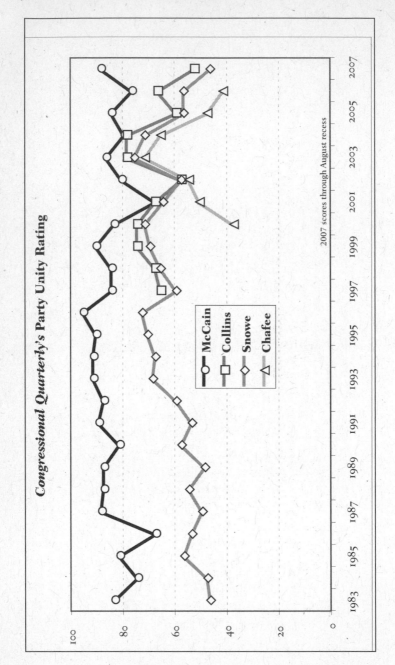

Congressional Quarterly's Party Unity Rating

2007 scores through August recess

The only years in which McCain diverged significantly from the Republican party line in the last two decades were 2001, when he voted with the party "only" 67 percent of the time, 2004, when he stuck to the party line 79 percent of the time, and 2006, when his unity score was 76. The rest of the time, throughout his nineteen-year Senate career, McCain has voted with his party more than 80 percent of the time in any given year. Again, a comparison with other senators described by the media as Republican moderates is instructive. In 2005, McCain voted with the party 84 percent of the time. Susan Collins's party unity rating was much lower, at 59 percent. Olympia Snowe's rating was even lower, at 56 percent. Meanwhile, Rhode Island's Lincoln Chafee actually voted with Democrats more often than Republicans, voting with his party only 47 percent of the time. Through the summer recess in 2007, McCain voted with his party 88 percent of the time, compared with Collins's 52 percent and Snowe's 46 percent.

Some might argue that McCain's slightly less conservative ratings in more recent years show that he is evolving into a true moderate. Forget for a moment that not even the most right-wing measure rates McCain as anything other than a safe conservative. The mistake made by those who want to believe he is a moderate is to assume that the McCain of 2001 and 2002 is the "real" John McCain. Never mind that those years, viewed in the context of his entire career, are outliers as far as his record goes. But even if we were to accept the premise, there is still plenty of cause for skepticism. For if we are to look at recent performance as an indicator of where a politician stands, shouldn't the same people who have given McCain the benefit of the doubt be concerned that 2005 and 2006 saw McCain veer away from his alleged moderation?

Liberal admirers of McCain like Jonathan Chait claim that McCain's recent efforts to court conservatives are merely an attempt at "repositioning himself from Bush-smiting champion of the center-left to Falwell-feting champion of the loony right."[58] Such a repositioning, says Chait, is actually a "not such a bad thing," as it will allow him to make it through the Republican primaries unscathed. Once past the primaries, the thinking goes, McCain can finally step out of the closet as the crusading progressive he really is. The operative assumption seems to be that when McCain goes along with the GOP agenda he is operating out of (sadly necessary) political expediency—not because he is calculating and manipulative, but because he has no other choice—but when he contradicts that agenda he is revealing his true self. But why is that McCain the real McCain, and not the other way around? As Charles Mahtesian wrote in the *National Journal*, "McCain isn't just inconveniently conservative on a few issues—he has been on the wrong side of virtually every issue of consequence to the Democratic Party over the past quarter-century."[59] Yet many moderates and even some liberals continue to believe that on the occasions when McCain does something they like, he is showing his "real" self. To them, the bulk of his record and history is merely a strategic feint meant to fool conservatives into voting for him, and once he wins he will revert to that "real" self and govern from the center. Interestingly enough, many tried-and-true conservatives believe the same thing, fueling suspicions about McCain despite his loyalty to their cause. The opinions of these two groups become mutually reinforcing: moderates take the antipathy of conservatives toward McCain as proof that their feelings about him are correct, and conservatives see moderates' affection for McCain the same way.

As if a lifetime's rhetoric and voting record were not enough, there are McCain's own testimonials about his allegiance. In his book *Worth the Fighting For*, McCain elaborates on the roots of his political philosophy: "No one had a more pronounced influence on my political convictions than Ronald Reagan. I embraced all of the core Reagan convictions. . . ."[60] He has hardly veered from that course. Telling a *Washington Post* reporter that he wouldn't jump ship to the other side in the 2004 election, he said, "I'm a Republican, a Teddy Roosevelt Republican, and while I admire the Democratic Party, I am committed to Republicans."[61] Mark Salter, McCain's chief of staff, recalled a conversation between McCain and Kerry where the Arizona senator had to remind the Democratic nominee why a mixed-party ticket wouldn't work. "We don't have the same philosophy. I'm a hawk, I'm for nation-building, I'm pro-life, I'm a free trader, I believe in small government," McCain said.[62] In the spring of 2006, responding to growing alarm among some liberal commentators that he was pandering to the GOP's base, he exclaimed, "I've always been a conservative. I think my voting record clearly indicates that on economic issues, national security issues, social issues—I'm pro-life—so I think I could make an argument I've had a pretty clear 20-some-year record basically being conservative."[63]

Off-Center

There is one more reason McCain is described so often as a centrist, one having less to do with McCain himself than with the political environment. McCain seems like more of a moderate now than he did at the beginning of his career not because he has changed his views on anything, but because the Republican Party has moved—and continues to move—to the right.

In their 2005 book *Off Center*, political scientists Jacob S. Hacker and Paul Pierson documented the growing radicalization of the Republican Party. Using the National Election Studies survey data compiled by the University of Michigan every election year, Hacker and Pierson found that the Republican base has grown increasingly conservative in the last forty years. In the 1960s, GOP activists—defined as people who identified with the Republican Party and participated in three or more election-related activities—were about 20 percent more conservative than independent voters. By 2002, however, they were a whopping 40 percent more conservative.

Yet even as the conservative base has moved further rightward, Americans in general have evinced little change in their political outlook. "Americans are about as liberal or conservative as they were a generation ago," argues political scientist Morris Fiorina, who conducted a study of the public's views on a host of polarizing issues.[64] Despite the influence of social conservatives within the GOP, American opinion has grown decidedly more progressive on many social issues in recent decades (such as gay rights and gender equality), while on other issues, such as abortion, opinions have barely budged in either direction. As Hacker and Pierson observe, "it is striking that across all of the major left-right issues, one is hard pressed to find *any* evidence that Americans are markedly more conservative today than they were in the recent (and even relatively distant) past."[65]

But the Republican base did move right, a move that was mirrored in the party's leadership. Drawing on the research of political economists Keith Poole and Howard Rosenthal, Hacker and Pierson found that today's congressional Republicans are far more conservative than they were twenty-five years ago. Poole and Rosenthal traced the votes of every congressperson who has ever served and constructed a measure to answer the question, how far to the right or left is an individual member of Congress? They then calculated the midpoint of all those measures for each congressional session. What they found was that the midpoint for the Republican Party has steadily moved to the right over the last three decades. Working with that research, Hacker and Pierson write:

> In the early 1970s, those in the middle of the House Republican delegation were approximately as conservative as current Republican Congressman Steven LaTourette of Ohio, whom the *Almanac of American Politics* notes has "the most moderate voting record of Ohio's Republican members." . . . Rather than a moderate like LaTourette, the typical GOP "centrist" in 2003 was someone like Congressman Mark Souder of Indiana—a one-time leader of the House Conservative Action Team, "an organization of fiscally and socially conservative House Republicans dedicated to protecting the traditional family, preserving mainstream American values, reducing the influence of the federal government, and respecting Congress' limited Constitutional authority."[66]

In other words, the Republican moderates of yesteryear were, in fact, fairly moderate. The Republican moderates in today's House, however, are actually pretty conservative.

The shift to the right has been even more dramatic in the Senate. In the early 1970s, the median position for Republican senators was pretty middle-of-the-road: significantly to the left of McCain and close to where Democrat Zell Miller stood before he retired in 2004. That has changed. The average Senate Republican in the early 2000s is about twice as conservative as the average Senate Republican in the early 1970s. Indeed, the average GOP Senate position today is just shy of that of former senator Rick Santorum—who before his 2006 defeat was considered a staunch conservative and favorite of the religious Right.

As for Senate Democrats, Hacker and Pierson demonstrate that they have moved to the left as well, though only by a seventh as much as their counterparts moved to the right. "In contrast with the common view, partisan polarization in Congress has not been caused by Republicans moving right and Democrats moving left in equal proportion," they write. "To the contrary, the right-ward shift of the GOP is the main cause of polarization."[67] In other words, a moderate Senate Democrat today is still that—a moderate—while a moderate Senate Republican is, in fact, very conservative. If the right-wing Santorum occupies the midpoint on the spectrum of contemporary Republicanism, it's no wonder that the decidedly conservative McCain can be plausibly presented as a moderate by the media.

When he first arrived in Washington over two decades ago, John McCain was a staunch Reagan Republican. In the intervening years, his ideology remained unchanged. But the media love moderates, and the media love mavericks. McCain surely came to understand that he could fit his square peg snugly into those round holes without moderating his actual positions on issues much at all. By carefully selecting issues on which the GOP's position was unpopular, he could make a well-publicized break with his party, win the admiration of reporters, and enhance his national stature at the same time. After a while the image would become self-perpetuating, as the press would seize on any break McCain made with other Republicans to give him attention that was priceless in both its volume and in the way it portrayed him. While other senators might work with the other party and be overlooked, McCain finds that when he does so, it guarantees him quotes in major newspapers, appearances on television, magazine profiles, and yet more reinforcement of the notion that he is a moderate, a centrist, an independent, and a maverick.

Chapter 6

Hopelessly Devoted

One might have thought that by the time John McCain began planning his second run for the presidency, his love affair with the media would have lost its spark. After all, McCain proved himself to be a loyal supporter of perhaps the most polarizing president in our history (and one of the least popular), and an unflagging advocate of a disastrous war that grew more unpopular by the day. Moreover, it has now been eight years since the Straight Talk Express barreled down the highways of New Hampshire, and it would be fair to expect that the excitement of the fling has waned in the intervening time.

Yet McCain set the stage for his 2008 presidential run, his relationship with the media showed few signs of changing. An effusive mash note by *Newsweek*'s Howard Fineman in mid-2005 summed up the continuing state of bliss between the senator and the press. Dubbing that summer "McCain's Moment," Fineman not only declared that McCain was somehow not a Republican, but stated outright that McCain and the media are engaged in some sort of common political enterprise: "Here in your nation's capital, three parties roam the landscape these days: Dobson-Rove Republicans, Reid-Pelosi Democrats and McCain-Media Independents."[1] Around the same time, a gushing profile of McCain appeared in the *New Yorker* titled "McCain's Party."[2] Sebastian Mallaby, writing in the *Washington Post* weeks later, hailed "McCainism," which he defined as a commitment to "good government" that somehow only McCain holds, as the country's only hope for deliverance from the mediocrity of the two major political parties.[3] Trudy Rubin of the *Philadelphia Inquirer* also hailed "McCainism," though she defined it as "a kind of straightforward authenticity."[4] Even the estimable E. J. Dionne acknowledged the pull of the McCain charm after all these years. After a perceptive dissection of how McCain breeds loyalty among journalists, Dionne wondered, "The question is whether McCain is playing a game with us" by courting reporters, "or whether the whole rap is real." He conceded, "What tilts me McCain's way—though not without reasonable doubts—is that he seems to have a well-developed view of human nature."[5]

Throughout their romance with John McCain, journalists have routinely given him the benefit of the doubt. As a result, nearly any political development seems to be interpreted as a boost to McCain. When Democrats won both houses of Congress in 2006, the *Washington Post* declared that it showed McCain's strength. "One of the secrets to the Democrats' success was winning over independents and moderates, exit polls showed. McCain has long been seen as a champion of independents," they wrote, contrasting him with Hillary Clinton.[6] Yet polls taken at the time asking about presidential preference found Clinton leading or tied with McCain. On the same day, the *Los Angeles Times* declared that the fact that two fiercely anti-immigrant Republican congressional candidates in Arizona lost meant that "the winner was John McCain." They neglected to mention that McCain had endorsed and campaigned for both candidates.[7] "What happened last Tuesday," said Mara Liasson on NPR's *Morning Edition*, "in particular, the role of independent and moderate voters, reinforces McCain's appeal as a general election candidate."[8] McCain's "strong national security credentials," said CNN's Bill Schneider a few days after the election, "are no small thing after a midterm where Iraq was a big issue."[9] Schneider didn't note that the election was if anything a repudiation of the Iraq war McCain boosted so consistently. The fact that McCain's position on the war at the time—send more troops—was supported by only 17 percent of 2006 voters, according to exit polls, didn't stop the *Washington Times* from running a front-page story the day after the election titled "McCain Gains Political Capital in Elections."[10]

Unsurprisingly, McCain's steps toward his 2008 candidacy were greeted in similar fashion. When he announced the formation of an exploratory committee shortly after the election, all the old tropes were trotted out. "Coming up," said CNN's Wolf Blitzer, "a maverick's major move, why Senator John McCain has virtually the entire political world, at least here in Washington, talking." Correspondent Candy Crowley said in the report that followed, "A hero in war, and a maverick in politics, the senator and his Straight Talk Express were the hit, if not the winner, of the 2000 election."[11] The *Los Angeles Times* noted, "Allies of McCain, whose maverick streak is thought to have cross-party appeal, say he is in the best position to thrive in the aftermath of election results that illustrated the GOP's weakness among independents."[12] *USA Today* agreed: "McCain, 70, was a prisoner of war in Vietnam. He showed appeal to moderates and independents in his bid for the 2000 GOP nomination against George W. Bush."[13] The *Christian Science Monitor* said, "McCain is now well-positioned to enhance his image as a maverick, triangulating between the Democratic-controlled Congress and the lame-duck Bush White House."[14]

But in 2006, McCain gave us even more material to question whether he really is the white knight of Washington that reporters have made him out to be. A litany of flip-flops and equivocations litters the Arizona senator's wake, as he has made an explicit show of his conservative views in a seeming attempt to pander to the right-wing base that will determine the winner of the GOP presidential primary. The result was something McCain hadn't experienced in some time: coverage that contained hints of criticism. But underneath it was the fundamental goodwill and presumption of good motives that the press has given McCain for the last decade.

True Colors

The year 2006 was busy for America's favorite senator. As in previous years, McCain was a ubiquitous presence in national life, the journalist's go-to guy for a pithy sound bite or a catchy comment. But with each passing week, the straight-talking maverick seemed to be giving way to someone different. Gone was the insurgent who said outrageous things to prick the establishment and win attention. In his place was a back-slapping insider, defending the administration at every turn, kowtowing to the base with little hesitation.

Where McCain began to get some uncomfortable questions was in his efforts to win the support of those on the hard right who had rallied to George W. Bush's side during the 2000 primaries. Perhaps the most publicized of McCain's gestures to pander to the right was his embrace of an old enemy, the since deceased Jerry Falwell. The reverend remained a major figure in the Republican Party and in the Christian conservative movement, a "kingmaker" who has also been responsible for some of the most virulent rhetoric to come from the Right. In the wake of 9/11, for instance, Falwell trained his sights on Americans:

> . . . what we saw on [9/11], as terrible as it is, could be minuscule if, in fact . . . God continues to lift the curtain and allow the enemies of America to give us probably what we deserve. The ACLU's got to take a lot of blame for this . . . I really believe that the pagans and the abortionists and the feminists and the gays and the lesbians who are actively trying to make that an alternative lifestyle . . . I point a finger in their face and say, "You helped this happen."[15]

Falwell later issued an unapologetic apology for his outburst, but there seems little doubt that the words conveyed his true feelings. When McCain singled out Falwell in 2000 as an "agent of intolerance,"[16] the senator was actually speaking the truth. Spoken with both eyes on the moderate middle, McCain's words nonetheless ended up backfiring on him. Bush had worked to make himself the candidate of conservative voters, and McCain's attempts to win over independents and moderate Republicans served to convince conservatives that Bush was their man. When McCain attacked Falwell and Pat Robertson, it only served to reinforce the idea among conservatives that he could not be trusted.

The fact that his 2000 campaign came up short mostly because of his inability to persuade conservative Republicans may well explain McCain's recent transformation into the president's staunchest defender—and the news in the fall of 2005 that McCain and Falwell had met face-to-face to bury the hatchet. The next March, the rapprochement was formalized when it was reported that McCain would give the commencement speech at Falwell's Liberty University. Moreover, the war of words between the two had turned into a mutual admiration society. Falwell in an interview said of McCain, "I've felt since I first knew about him that he stood on the right side of the ball on social issues. I don't think he has changed his views. He is certainly pro-life. He clearly is an advocate of the husband-female family, he does not support same-sex marriage. I know of no reason I could not support him."[17] He also said that McCain told him that he had spoken in haste in his condemnation of Falwell and fellow Christian conservative Pat Robertson during his 2000 campaign. McCain's speech at Liberty was not too different from the commencement speeches he has given on many occasions—albeit with more references to God, and a plea for those who disagree about politics to grant others goodwill. Later, McCain would hire the coach of Liberty's champion debate team to work on his 2008 presidential campaign.

McCain was in no less of a hurry than Falwell to leave their prior conflicts in the past. In April, appearing on NBC's *Meet the Press*, McCain made what can only be described as a blatant flip-flop. Host Tim Russert asked about McCain's recent reconciliatory gestures toward Falwell. "We, we agreed to disagree on certain issues and we agreed to move forward," McCain told

Russert. The host read a passage from Falwell's odious 9/11 statement and asked McCain, "Are you embracing that?" McCain replied that he was only going to give a graduation speech at Falwell's school and did not necessarily embrace all of his beliefs, just as he did not agree with all the values of other universities at which he had delivered speeches. "Do you believe that Jerry Falwell is still an agent of intolerance?" pressed Russert. "No, I don't," McCain replied, adding petulantly, "I think that Jerry Falwell can explain to you his views on this program when you have him on." Russert then broached the subtext:

> RUSSERT: Are you concerned that people are going to say, "I see John McCain tried 'straight talk express,' 'maverick,' it didn't work out in 2000, so now in 2008, he's going to become a conventional, typical politician, reaching out to people that he called agents of intolerance, voting for tax cuts he opposed, to make himself more appealing to the hard-core Republican base."
>
> McCAIN: I think most people will judge my record exactly for what it is, where I take positions that I stand, that I stand for and I believe in.[18]

And Falwell was not the only religious Right leader to whom McCain paid respect. In early 2007, McCain met with San Antonio evangelist John Hagee to express a "shared commitment to the state of Israel."[19] Hagee is hardly a mainstream religious figure—he has argued, for instance, that a war with Iran is desirable and necessary to help bring about Armageddon and the Second Coming, and that the Antichrist will be the head of the European Union.[20]

McCain's reply to Russert presupposes that people know what

exactly he believes in—which is hardly a given. Take his stand on the Bush tax cuts. The alleged closet progressive was hailed by the media for his stance against Bush's enormous 2001 tax cut package, which overwhelmingly benefited the rich and contributed to the transformation of the budget surplus into a deficit. And yet, in 2006, when those tax cuts went up for an extension and with McCain in need of demonstrating his right-wing bona fides, McCain voted with his Senate Republican colleagues to keep them on the books. Even tax-cutting advocates who cheered McCain's reversal could not help but call it for what it was. "It's a big flip-flop," said Grover Norquist, "but I'm happy that he's flopped."[21]

Taxes are not the only area in which McCain turned his back on previously stated positions as 2008 approached. On abortion, McCain's statements have hardly been a model of clarity. When he was asked about the potential repeal of *Roe v. Wade* in January 2006, he said, "I've never agreed with *Roe v. Wade*, so it wouldn't bother me any."[22] But he had opposed repealing the decision in the past. In an interview with the *San Francisco Chronicle* in 1999, McCain said, "I'd love to see a point where [*Roe vs. Wade*] is irrelevant, and could be repealed because abortion is no longer necessary. But certainly in the short term, or even the long term, I would not support repeal of *Roe vs. Wade*, which would then force X number of women in America to [undergo] illegal and dangerous operations."[23] Two days later, in an appearance on CNN, McCain said, "I favor the ultimate repeal of *Roe v. Wade*. But we all know, and it's obvious, that if we repeal *Roe v. Wade* tomorrow, thousands of young American women would be performing [*sic*] illegal and dangerous operations."[24] McCain seemed to be arguing that he would favor repealing *Roe*, but only once America somehow reached the point at which no one needed or wanted an abortion. Still receiving fire from anti-abortion forces, two days after his

CNN appearance, McCain wrote a letter to the National Right to Life Committee stating, "I share our common goal of reducing the staggering number of abortions currently performed in this country and overturning the Roe vs. Wade decision."[25] Then, at a small rally, he told the crowd, "The issue of abortion is incredibly difficult and I believe life begins at conception." But then he went on: "I also want the Republican Party to be an inclusive party . . . and we cannot impose a litmus test on the issue." This prompted one pro-life woman to say, "This wasn't straight talk. He was evasive." A pro-choice activist wasn't happy either, accusing McCain of being on "both sides of the issue."[26]

As 2008 approached, McCain's position on *Roe* remained fuzzy. When in 2006 Republicans in South Dakota passed a draconian abortion ban, making all abortions illegal except those that would save the life of the mother, McCain was asked by the Washington tip sheet the *Hotline* what he would have done had he been governor of the state. His office replied that McCain "would have signed the legislation, but would also take the appropriate steps under state law—in whatever state—to ensure that the exceptions of rape, incest or life of the mother were included."[27] But of course, the absence of the first two exceptions was exactly what made the South Dakota law so controversial. McCain's statement would not have been any different from saying, "I would favor overturning *Roe v. Wade*, as long as *Roe v. Wade* were not overturned." His odd position on the South Dakota law was, with a couple of exceptions, including Dick Polman of the *Philadelphia Inquirer*, mostly ignored by the national press. For good measure, Falwell gave McCain's abortion stance his thumbs-up. "Most of the pro-life community, myself included, is happy with McCain's pro-life views,"[28] said Falwell.

By the end of the year, McCain was coming out far more

clearly for repealing *Roe*. Appearing on ABC's *This Week* on November 19, he said, "I believe that we would be better off by having *Roe v. Wade* returned to the states. And I don't believe the Supreme Court should be legislating in the way that they did on *Roe v. Wade*."[29] To clarify, repealing *Roe* is what would be necessary to "return" the issue of abortion "to the states." As the primaries drew closer, he became more categorical. "I do not support *Roe versus Wade*," he told a South Carolina audience in February 2007. "It should be overturned."[30]

For a different politician, McCain's bobbing and weaving on abortion over the years would have been described as straddling, waffling, or worse—the calculating politician calibrating his beliefs to ingratiate himself with the constituency at hand. That was the press verdict on Al Gore after critics in 2000 noted that his position on abortion had changed over the years. And after Senator Hillary Clinton gave a 2005 speech restating her long-held view that abortion should be "safe, legal, and rare," some pundits accused her of being "transparent"[31] and taking a "poll-tested path,"[32] despite the fact that the formulation had been a consistent part of Democratic rhetoric on the issue for over a decade. The speech was cited again and again whenever a journalist or commentator wanted to show that Clinton was "moving to the center," evidence that she was massaging her actual views for political advantage. Yet McCain's varying statements on abortion haven't seemed to diminish his reputation for straight talk.

Another subject near and dear to the base's heart is gay marriage. For much of his career, McCain has been successfully non-committal on gay issues. His cannily soothing rhetoric on gay rights—for instance, he said in 2000 that he would be happy to appoint gay staffers to his administration—has led many to assume that he is at least a moderate on the subject. In 2004, McCain spoke out against a federal anti–gay marriage amendment as "antithetical in every way to the core philosophy of Republicans."[33] But as his rapprochement with the Right gathered steam in 2006, McCain began to look and sound more like the conservative Republican that he is. In 2005, McCain backed—and appeared in ads in support of—an Arizona ballot initiative amending the state constitution to define marriage as a union between a man and a woman and denying government benefits to unmarried couples (the measure failed at the ballot box). McCain also opposes the Employment Non-Discrimination Act, which would ban discrimination on the basis of sexual orientation in the workplace. "I don't believe we should discriminate against anyone in the workplace," said McCain, "but I don't think we need specific laws that would apply necessarily to people who are gay."[34] In other words, he opposes discrimination, but he also opposes banning discrimination. And in his conversation with Jerry Falwell, McCain "reconfirmed" that he would support a constitutional amendment defining marriage as solely between a man and a woman were a federal court to strike down state bans on gay marriage.[35]

Science has been another casualty of McCain's rightward tack. In a 2005 interview with the editors of the *Arizona Daily Star*, McCain revealed his evolving views on "intelligent design," a pseudoscientific notion devised by creationists as a tool to undermine the teaching of evolution. In 2000, McCain had declared that the teaching of intelligent design was a matter for local school boards to decide, in contrast to George W. Bush's belief that creationism itself should be taught in classrooms. In 2005, however, McCain expressed more openness to the idea of intelligent design, saying that "different schools of thought" about the origins of mankind should be presented to students. Interestingly, this response mirrored what President Bush had said just three weeks earlier, when he defended the teaching of intelligent design by saying, "I think that part of education is to expose people to different schools of thought."[36] When asked whether intelligent design belonged in a science class, McCain responded, "Well, there's enough scientists that believe that it does. . . . This is something that I think all point of views should be presented."[37]

Contrary to McCain's claim, the scientific community has in fact rejected intelligent design as a credible scientific theory. In 2002, the American Association for the Advancement of Science (AAAS) published a resolution in which the organization determined that proponents of intelligent design had "failed to offer credible scientific evidence to support their claim that ID [intelligent design] undermines the current scientifically accepted theory of evolution," and had not "proposed a scientific means of testing its claims." Having reached those conclusions, the AAAS determined "that the lack of scientific warrant for so-called 'intelligent design theory' makes it improper to include as a part of science education."[38]

It is fair to say that few of McCain's flip-flops have seemed as motivated by political considerations as his reversal on the issue of ethanol subsidies. In 2000, McCain decided not to compete in the Iowa caucus and focused his attention on New Hampshire, a decision that turned out to be a good one. One problem he knew he would face in Iowa was that he had opposed federal subsidies for the production of ethanol, an alternative fuel made from corn, which is abundant in Iowa. Whatever the merits of ethanol, one of the less savory aspects of the presidential primaries is the way senators and governors suddenly adopt a deep and abiding interest in the substance as the Iowa caucus approaches. In 2000,

McCain's unwillingness to go along with this quadrennial parade of pandering was just one more indication that he was a maverick and an independent. He criticized the subsidies and the substance itself, even after the campaign was over. "Ethanol does nothing to reduce fuel consumption, nothing to increase our energy independence, nothing to improve air quality," McCain said in 2003.[39]

But unlike in 2000, McCain decided he could not skip the Iowa caucuses in 2008. By a fortuitous coincidence, his position on ethanol underwent a transformation. "I support ethanol and I think it is a vital, a vital alternative energy source not only because of our dependency on foreign oil but its greenhouse gas reduction effects," he said in a speech in Iowa in August 2006.[40] McCain's reason? He has said his anti-ethanol position softened when oil hit $40 per barrel. Although he never explained why he picked $40 per barrel as a benchmark, his reasoning would make more sense were it not for the fact that in June 2005, when oil was at $60 per barrel, McCain's office put out a press release opposing ethanol mandates in the 2005 Energy Bill. The release went so far as to say that the mandates would result in higher gas prices.

Yet when McCain's ethanol flip-flop is discussed, it is generally raised as a comment on the nature of the presidential campaign, not as evidence that McCain is an insincere panderer. One *Washington Post* article from March 2007 spent nearly all of its 1,230 words tracing Hillary Clinton's various statements and votes on the issue. "Political opponents depict Clinton's about-face as pandering to Iowa Democrats," the article said, yet it spent only a few sentences on McCain, saying he was "an ethanol foe so fierce that he skipped the Iowa caucuses in 2000," who now "says he is willing to give it another look."

Barely a Backlash

It was hard to ignore McCain's startling public pirouette that began in early 2005. The transformation has been so obvious that some in the media actually began to take notice. Ron Fournier of the Associated Press led an April 2006 McCain profile with, "Has the 'Straight Talk Express' veered to the right?"[41] Writing in the *New York Times*, Adam Nagourney reported that McCain "is *portraying himself* [emphasis added] as a lifelong conservative and a steadfast supporter of President Bush," the kind of skeptical language usually applied to other politicians but not McCain.[42]

A smattering of liberal pundits blew the whistle on the Arizona senator in the wake of his efforts to court the Republican establishment and far-right figures like Falwell, some arguing that McCain was turning his back on his prior beliefs and some contending that the entire "maverick" persona was never real to begin with. The *New York Times*'s Paul Krugman opined, "It's time for some straight talk about John McCain. He isn't a moderate. He's much less of a maverick than you'd think. And he isn't the straight talker he claims to be."[43] In response, ABCNews.com's "The Note"—the pitch-perfect expression of the Washington journalistic conventional wisdom—huffed that "Krugman writes *with selective facts* [emphasis added] that John McCain is not a maverick, a moderate, nor a straight talker."[44] Unsurprisingly, "The Note" itself offered no facts, selective or otherwise, to refute Krugman. E. J. Dionne, writing in the *Washington Post*, warned, "If McCain spends the next two years obviously positioning himself to win Republican primary votes, he will start to look just like another politician. Once lost, a maverick's image is hard to earn back."[45] Even Dionne's criticism was tinged with sadness, however, as he admitted to missing the unconventional and interesting McCain the media used to know and love.

Appearing on *The Daily Show with Jon Stewart*, McCain was questioned about his cozying up to Falwell. "You're killin' me here," Stewart said to McCain regarding his upcoming Liberty University speech. "I feel like it's a condoning of Falwell's kind of crazy-making to some extent to have you go down there, and it strikes me as something you wouldn't normally do. Am I wrong about that?" McCain responded with his boilerplate retort about giving speeches at all kinds of schools whose values might differ from his. Stewart, though clearly sympathetic to McCain, ended the interview by asking, "Are you going into crazy base world?" to which the senator could only meekly respond, "I'm afraid so."[46]

These criticisms aside, the media's love for McCain has hardly dimmed in the wake of his reconciliation with the Right. The image of the senator as a moderate, even a progressive, still persists in the mainstream media, perpetuated by a press corps relying on ancient and inaccurate story lines. One of the worst offenders in this regard is MSNBC's Chris Matthews, who may be the head of the McCain fan club among the establishment press. Matthews has said, "I'm still hanging in there for a McCain-Giuliani ticket,"[47] and even admitted in September 2006, "The press loves McCain. We're his base."[48] When Gloria Borger said on Matthews's show that McCain is a reformer, Matthews replied, "So he's kind of like Martin Luther."[49] On a January 2007 edition of *Hardball*, Chris Matthews asked about Hillary Clinton, "What have you done to deserve this job?" When his guest said that the question was "a tough question not just for her, for perhaps the entire field," Matthews interrupted him. "Not so much for McCain," he said. "He has deserved the presidency. Whether he should be president or not, it's up to the voters. But he's certainly done a lot."[50] Three months later, Matthews made the point again: "I think the guy deserves to be president in terms of all his service to the country."[51]

Hardly a mention of McCain goes by without Matthews blurting out the word "maverick." In a string of appearances in March 2006, Matthews may well have broken some sort of record on the uses of the word "maverick" and its variations in discussing John McCain's appearance at the Southern Republican Leadership Conference on March 10. Matthews referred to McCain as "a maverick,"[52] "kind of . . . a maverick,"[53] "a solo fighter pilot out there,"[54] "kind of a party renegade,"[55] and a "lone gun."[56]

And what was it that Matthews was praising so highly? McCain's praise of George W. Bush. "The fate of the world may hang in the balance and we should all of us keep our personal ambitions a distant second to standing with the president of the United States, our commander in chief," proclaimed McCain at the convention. Facing a straw poll he knew he was likely to lose to Tennessean Bill Frist (the convention was held in Memphis), McCain came up with a brilliant solution. "Straw polls are entertaining, my friends, even extremely early ones, but I think we have bigger things to worry about. So if any friends are thinking about voting for me, please don't. Just write in President Bush's name," said McCain.[57] His statement not only made it possible to dismiss his eventual loss in the straw poll, it demonstrated to Republican activists his fealty to Bush—two birds killed with one deftly tossed stone.

But without irony, Matthews pointed to McCain's tribute to Bush as a case study of the maverick in action. Another pundit, Chuck Todd, made the same point on Matthews's show. Appearing on *Hardball*, Todd, the editor of the *Hotline* (who would later become political director of NBC News), said that McCain's support for Bush was quintessential McCain because "rallying around the president is the maverick thing to do."[58] A year later, after he had become political director of NBC News, Todd once again found McCain's willingness to support the president (and agree with nearly all his Republican colleagues) to be the essence of maverickness. "It would be easy for him to criticize the war," Todd said on the *Today* show. "The maverick thing to do is to actually take the unpopular stand."[59] Witness the logic at work: When McCain challenges Bush, it is proof that he is a maverick. When he cozies up to Bush, it is also proof of the same.

McCain's reputation as an advocate for reform and good government also continues to overshadow his deeds. In a segment on *Good Morning America*, ABC's Jake Tapper said that John McCain is "such an opponent of pork he's almost kosher."[60] Even more effusive was a profile in *Time* naming him one of America's ten best senators, crediting him for spending "his entire Senate career exposing wasteful pork-barrel projects" and describing him as "a waste and fraud hunter."[61] In lauding McCain, such media outlets conveniently overlooked contradictory evidence, such as a bill McCain proposed calling for $10 million in federal money to establish a center at the University of Arizona law school as a tribute to the late Supreme Court chief justice William H. Rehnquist, a proposal that has been derided by critics as "a classic case of lawmakers' trying to funnel money directly to a home-state institution for a project that should find financing elsewhere."[62]

Such tributes also failed to take into account McCain's questionable record on corruption issues, particularly with regard to disgraced former Republican lobbyist Jack Abramoff. As early as March 2005, *Roll Call* reported that McCain had assured colleagues Senator Conrad Burns (R-MT) and Senator David Vitter (R-LA) that they would not be caught up in the Senate Indian

Affairs Committee investigation into how Abramoff bilked $82 million from the American Indian tribes he represented. "We stop when we find out where the money went," McCain said.[63] But one of the places the money went was to John McCain. He received $5,000 in contributions from the Mississippi Band of Choctaw, one of Abramoff's clients. McCain has also been documented as a recipient of donations from clients of Abramoff's. When Democrats were revealed to have similar relationships with Abramoff clients, reporters characterized them as tainted. With McCain, however, the relationship with Abramoff clients has simply been ignored—sometimes in the same article. *Newsweek*'s Howard Fineman, for instance, characterized "lawmakers fingered by the feds in Abramoff probe, or who received campaign contributions through the networking of Abramoff" as "losers" in the scandal, while the "winners" included John McCain, whom Fineman envisioned "leading an independent effort to 'clean up' the capital as a third-party candidate." Fineman didn't mention McCain's contributions from Abramoff clients.[64]

McCain's hollow record on reform goes beyond the Abramoff mess. In a March issue of the *Hill* newspaper, reporter Alexander Bolton revealed that McCain, in recent months, had taken less interest in reform issues. Bolton wrote, "McCain's lower-than-hoped-for profile on the sensitive subject [of lobbying reform] coincides with what prominent lobbyists describe as a quiet effort by his political team to court inside-the-Beltway donors."[65]

Perhaps no recent incident underscored the media's reflexive resort to established story lines than McCain's dust-up with Democratic Senator Barack Obama (IL). In early February 2006, the two senators were involved in a highly publicized dispute over lobbying reform. It was precipitated by Obama's decision to part ways with McCain on the issue, pushing for a reform bill put forward by Democratic Party leaders instead of supporting McCain's initiative to form a bipartisan task force to come up with a reform plan. Obama reasoned—rightly—that a task force would only slow the momentum for lobbying reform and dilute the proposal engineered by then–Senate minority leader Harry Reid (NV). But to McCain, Obama's decision was nothing less than a personal blow—the neophyte showing up the iconic reformer. In a caustic letter (immediately given to the press, of course), McCain slammed Obama for turning his back on what he construed as a commitment to McCain's proposal and for "self-interested partisan posturing." "I have been around long enough to appreciate that in politics, the public interest isn't always a priority for every one of us," McCain wrote. When asked by reporters to comment on the contretemps, McCain dubbed his letter "a little straight talk."

McCain's lashing out at Obama shouldn't have been too surprising. As the *Boston Globe*'s Walter Robinson (notably, one of the few national reporters to investigate George W. Bush's National Guard service during the 2000 campaign) observed in 1999, this kind of incident was familiar to people involved in Arizona politics. "It is not so much the temper, they say, but what prompts him to lose it: His frequent unwillingness to accommodate dissenting views, even those of average citizens; his sometimes bullying insistence that other politicians do his bidding; and his tendency to treat those who disagree with him as disloyal."[66] Whether the fact that Obama deprived McCain of the opportunity to take the spotlight for another "bipartisan" effort played a part, we cannot say.

The spectacle of two high-profile senators going mano a mano was irresistible to the media. While Obama, like McCain, has received positive coverage from the Washington press, it was clear whose side of the story they were favoring. On CBS's *Evening News*, Gloria Borger uncritically presented McCain's accusations of partisanship against Obama, while adding, "It's very clear that lobbying reform is a very personal issue for John McCain. It's very important to John McCain."[67] On CNN, congressional correspondent Ed Henry stated, "McCain, who's long pushed reform, didn't take kindly to the lecture from a freshman." On the same episode, Stuart Rothenberg, editor and publisher of the *Rothenberg Political Report*, asserted that the dispute could allow McCain to "reassert his ownership of the ethics issue."[68] Chris Matthews asked McCain, "Did [Obama] welsh on the deal? Did he double-cross you by going partisan after promising to go bipartisan with you?"[69] And so went the reports, which defined the dispute as that between a true reformer (McCain) and an upstart senator looking to politicize the issue (Obama).

What they left out was the fact that Obama's rationale for sticking with the Democratic plan was actually sound. Far from "partisan," as McCain accused him of being, Obama opted to pursue ethics reform via the regular committee process rather than through an ad hoc task force—a reasonable choice for someone dedicated to meaningful reform rather than a showy facsimile of it. The press also allowed McCain to depict Obama as a politicking grandstander, when it was in fact McCain, with his self-aggrandizing mention of straight talk and the public release of his letter scolding Obama, who was playing the incident up for maximum political benefit. As Mark Schmitt wrote in the *American Prospect*, "McCain, with the help of an adoring press, essentially defined and controlled the concept of 'bipartisanship.'"[70] The dispute with Obama was less about pushing through effective reform than McCain zealously guarding his monopoly on bipartisanship. That the Democratic proposal could lead to stronger reform was unimportant; all that mattered was that whatever reform came out of Congress, McCain the bipartisan reformer could claim credit for it.

Months later, Chris Matthews recalled the incident in an interview with McCain, characterizing it once again as a heroic McCain victory, in terms even McCain himself could barely stomach:

> MATTHEWS: Didn't you call him out once? I remember you called him out and he buckled.
>
> McCAIN: No, he didn't. But I have worked with him—
>
> MATTHEWS: Yes, he did.
>
> McCAIN: I have worked with him—
>
> MATTHEWS: Yes, he did.
>
> McCAIN: No, he didn't. I have worked with him on a—
>
> MATTHEWS: He folded, he folded. You were the tough guy!
>
> McCAIN: Stop.[71]

While Matthews may be McCain's most embarrassingly effusive booster in the media, McCain also receives steady praise from those pundits who inhabit the bland center of conventional wisdom, best embodied by the *Washington Post*'s David Broder. In a May 2006 column, Broder had this to say about McCain: "The presumption of authenticity—the assumption that what he says, he actually believes—is John McCain's greatest strength going into the 2008 presidential race."[72] It wasn't the first time Broder praised McCain's "authenticity." After the 2004 election, he wrote that the senator's popularity could be attributed to "McCain's success in satisfying the widespread public hunger for authenticity and candor in political leaders. The name he gave his campaign bus in 2000, 'The Straight Talk Express,' perfectly captured what voters now see in him—the rare Washington official who says what he thinks and lets the chips fall where they may."[73] Broder isn't the only pundit to tout McCain's authenticity. Mike Allen of the *Politico* (and formerly of *Time* magazine and the *Washington Post*) told conservative talk show host Glenn Beck in early 2007, "I think that people want someone who's honest, candid. They're tired of the pabulum . . . It's why people in the past have liked Senator John McCain. Authenticity."[74]

A corollary to the authenticity trope is the acceptance among reporters that McCain's unmistakable pandering to the Right is an unfortunate but understandable strategy that McCain needs to undertake in order to win the Republican nomination. According to this line of thinking, the maverick is only suppressing his moderate, independent ways for a spell. Once past the nomination process, the real, more moderate McCain will return.

To his liberal advocates, McCain's conservative position–taking can be dismissed for the same reason as his personal courting of right-wing figures like Jerry Falwell: he's just doing what he has to do. As Jonathan Chait of the *New Republic* wrote, "Go ahead, senator, flip-flop away. I know you're with us at heart."[75] (In fairness to Chait, he later recanted on McCain, comparing him to Darth Vader: "But over time, his pursuit of power became the goal itself, and by the end he lost his capacity to differentiate between right and wrong."[76]) Jacob Weisberg, writing in *Slate*, said that McCain's critics on the left who assail his recent 180-degree turns on issues have McCain pegged wrong. "This is a stratagem—the only one, in fact, that gives him a shot at surviving a Republican presidential primary," he writes.[77] Even ostensibly critical articles, such as Nagourney's, which was quoted above, operate on the presumption that the Arizona senator has been hiding his deepest, truest self in recent months in an understandable effort to win the party's nomination. To the media, the John McCain of 2000, 2001, and 2002 is all that matters, negating more than two decades of ardent conservatism, both in the years prior to and after the maverick's heyday. But was that McCain more real than Bush the compassionate conservative? Is it possible that the real John McCain, lifelong Republican, avowed keeper of the Reagan flame, is closer to the 2006 version than the 2000 candidate that reporters fell in love with? Chait called McCain's recent conservative drift a "fake right." But is it any less plausible that it was, in fact, McCain's courting of the middle beginning in 2000 that was a "fake left"?

Yet some remain convinced that if he ever wins the White House, McCain will show himself to be something other than what his career to this point would indicate. (Apparently, that was John Kerry's assumption when he toyed with offering McCain his vice presidential nomination in 2004.) One suspects that they see personal qualities they admire in McCain and conclude that he must therefore share their ideology as well, at least to some extent. The *New Republic* is a particularly notable outpost of adulation for McCain; in addition to printing Michael Lewis's admiring articles during the 2000 campaign and Chait's praise for the Arizona senator, the magazine ran a cover story by John Judis in October 2006 lamenting—not attacking, but lamenting—McCain's neoconservative views on foreign policy. "I have liked John McCain ever since I met him almost a decade ago," begins the piece, which goes on to describe the many ways in which McCain is better than ordinary politicians. He is a "rarity in Washington: a centrist by conviction rather than design," someone possessed of "one other attribute that separates him from many of his peers in Washington: He is willing to change his mind."[78]

Ordinary politicos might move to the center as a political maneuver, or flip-flop for expediency's sake, but not McCain. And if he is wrong on an issue, many liberals say hopefully, just give him time and he'll come around. *Slate*'s Jacob Weisberg responded to McCain's overtures to the Right by describing him as "a social progressive, a fiscal conservative, and a military hawk. Should he triumph in the primaries, we can expect this more appealing John McCain to come roaring back." Weisberg dismissed McCain's support of an anti-gay initiative in Arizona, saying his readers "should be sophisticated enough to recognize that politics is the art of the possible, and that what's in McCain's heart on this subject (as President Bush might say) is not a viable stance for any presidential candidate just yet, especially a Republican one."[79] Exactly how he knew the contents of McCain's heart—not to mention why those contents should matter more than what McCain actually does and says on the public stage—Weisberg did not say. A few months later, liberal columnist Eleanor Clift noted that Arizona had just voted down the initiative, but omitted the fact that McCain not only supported it but cut television advertisements urging Arizonans to vote in favor. "McCain gets more latitude on this subject because we sense that in his heart, he's a Goldwater libertarian," Clift wrote (Goldwater advocated allowing gays to serve in the military, among other things). "Social issues are not what drive him in public life. He's playing to his party's conservative base as newly defined by the religious right, but if elected president, he's not going to be beholden to them the way Bush has been."[80]

We noted previously how McCain has been able to wipe away all manner of political sins merely by offering reporters statements of regret, thus maintaining his image as a man of unimpeachable principle. Likewise, McCain is astute enough to realize that he can maintain his maverick credentials even when he engages in blatant pandering, simply by signaling to reporters that he feels bad about it. So the *Washington Post*'s David Ignatius will write a column about McCain's nascent presidential campaign in early 2006 in which he argues, "A successful campaign almost requires some fibbing—the candidate is either less extreme than he's telling his party's base, or more extreme than he's telling the general public." So is McCain just the same as any other candidate? Not to Ignatius: "A McCain candidacy, if he makes the formal decision next year to run, will be rooted in his image as a man of principle. But it will also be something of a balancing act—one that the candidate himself is likely to find uncomfortable." When McCain acts like other politicians, it is not evidence that he might be, well, like other politicians. Instead, the focus is on how uncomfortable it makes him (the piece was titled, "A Man Who Won't Sell His Soul"[81]). Try to find an example of a centrist columnist like Ignatius writing about how a politician like Bill Clinton, Al Gore, or John Kerry had no choice but to pander to his party's base—yet using that as evidence of the politician's strong character.

Indeed, as McCain's efforts to win acceptance from the right wing of the Republican Party and assume the mantle of establishment candidate became clearer, those who wrote about it often adopted this tone, one more of sorrow than of anger (much less contempt). In a ten-thousand-word profile in *Vanity Fair* in early 2007 entitled "Prisoner of Conscience," former *New York Times* reporter Todd Purdum laid out many of the less than honorable things McCain was doing in his second quest for the White House, but the message was unmistakable: John McCain may be engaging in pandering, dishonesty, and hypocrisy, but it's tearing him up inside. "The biggest questions of all," Purdum wrote, "are whether, by forcing himself to become some kind of something he just isn't, John McCain can win the presidency to begin with, and would he consider himself to be worthy of the honor if he did." The piece ended this way:

> McCain's own compromises in pursuit of the presidency may be necessary, even justified. And they may, in fact, pave his way to victory in the Republican primaries, and perhaps to the White House itself. But even if no one calls him out, and the public plays along, McCain may pay an awful price. Because, whatever happens, he will know. He will know. He will know.[82]

Here again we see how different the rules are for John McCain. When an ordinary politician does something the journalist or columnist finds objectionable, we are often told that he has revealed his true self. But when John McCain does something that writers like Ignatius and Purdum find objectionable, they tell us that McCain has not revealed his true (flawed) self, but betrayed his true (good) self.

Here, There, and Everywhere

"Sometimes the power of a law depends on the lawmaker," wrote *Time* magazine when in 2006 they declared John McCain to be one of America's ten best senators. "Last May the Senate unanimously passed a Democratic amendment banning the torture of prisoners in U.S. custody. No one paid any attention. Then in October Republican John McCain introduced his antitorture amendment, using identical language, and the issue made headlines in newspapers across the country . . . It wasn't just that McCain, 69, had been tortured as a prisoner of war in Vietnam. McCain has that rare ability to put an issue on the U.S. agenda that wouldn't naturally be there."[83]

Just what is this "rare ability" of which *Time* spoke? In truth, it isn't his ability alone. McCain didn't garner headlines by virtue of some magical power he possesses to bend printing presses to his will. Headlines don't just happen, they are the result of decisions made by journalists. When the Senate passed the Democratic amendment on torture, journalists *chose* to ignore it, just as they *chose* to give play to McCain's amendment (and as they chose to ignore the "signing statement" President Bush issued on signing the law, in which he effectively declared that he would not enforce it).

As the *Time* story suggests, when John McCain does or says something, journalists consider it "news" in a way they don't for most of his colleagues. The result is that, even apart from the positivity of the coverage he receives, McCain has reaped political benefit from simply being everywhere. Media ubiquity has contributed to his elevation to colossus status in American politics. According to the *Hotline*'s "White House '08 Watch," a tally of how much television time all the presumptive candidates for the 2008 presidential election receive, John McCain was the most omnipresent presidential hopeful on TV. From September 2005 to December 2006, McCain appeared on broadcast and cable television for a total of over twenty-one hours, far more than any other presidential candidate.

McCain's ubiquity can also be quantified by the number of times he has been mentioned in the press compared with other high-profile politicians. A Nexis search of all news outlets in 2006 finds that McCain led all political figures in mentions, with 33,683. Compare that with Biden, who, despite being on TV more times than any other Democrat, was mentioned only 8,107 times during the same year. Hillary Clinton, by far the most mentioned Democrat, appeared in stories 24,288 times, over 9,000 fewer mentions

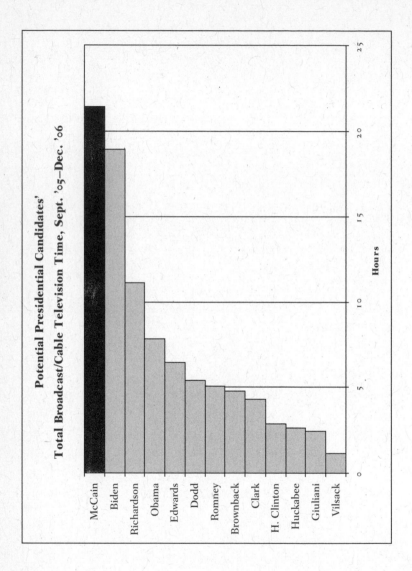

Potential Presidential Candidates'
Total Broadcast/Cable Television Time, Sept. '05–Dec. '06

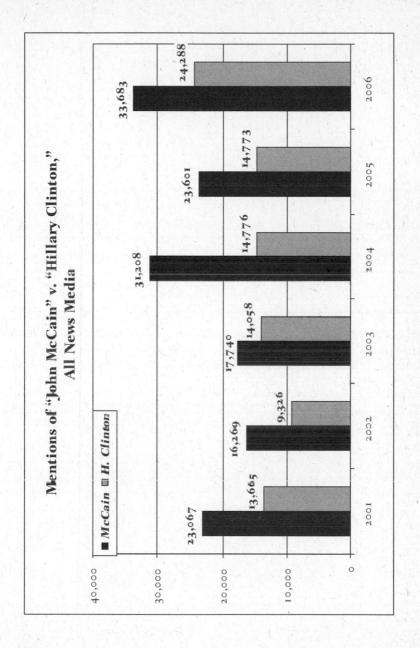

Mentions of "John McCain" v. "Hillary Clinton,"
All News Media

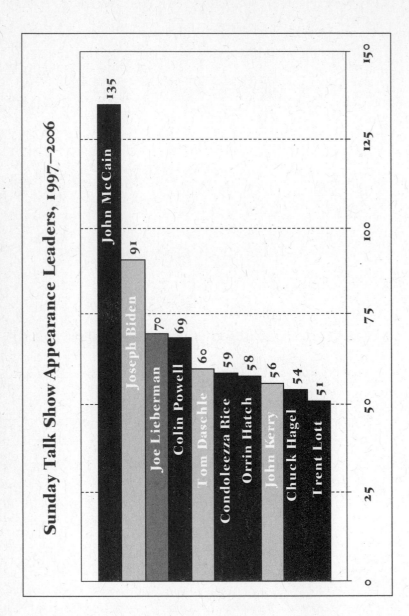

Sunday Talk Show Appearance Leaders, 1997–2006

John McCain 135
Joseph Biden 91
Joe Lieberman 70
Colin Powell 69
Tom Daschle 60
Condoleezza Rice 59
Orrin Hatch 58
John Kerry 56
Chuck Hagel 54
Trent Lott 51

than McCain. It's no surprise really, as McCain has trumped Clinton in press mentions since she came to the Senate in January 2001.

The same holds true for the dispensers of conventional wisdom that are the Sunday morning talk shows. A Media Matters for America study found that between 1997 and 2006, John McCain was by far the most frequent guest on *Meet the Press*, *Face the Nation*, and *This Week*. Over that period, McCain appeared as a guest 135 times, far outpacing the runner-up, Joe Biden, who tallied 91 appearances.

Moreover, McCain has had the benefit of usually appearing solo on those shows, instead of sharing the time with someone from across the partisan or ideological aisle. When a guest is interviewed alone by the host of a Sunday show, the networks send a message that what the person says is so important that it needs to be presented with no contradiction or interruption from a fellow guest. In McCain's case, the solo appearances can also be seen as a ratification of his media-made reputation as standing above the petty back-and-forth of partisan politics—he's so independent and fair minded that he requires no countervailing opinions to balance his own. Fully 72 percent of McCain's Sunday-show guest spots over this ten-year period were solo gigs—including all eleven of his appearances in 2006. With ninety-seven solo guest appearances during the period, McCain easily bests Biden, who came in a distant second, appearing by himself thirty times.[84]

The perpetuation of complimentary motifs designed by McCain and his advisers ("maverick," "straight talk"), the obfuscation of his conservative record, his ubiquity on air and in print—all of these continue to define the media's handling of John McCain. For a time, there was a feeling that McCain, should he manage to win the Republican nomination in 2008, would be all but unbeatable. As *Slate*'s Mickey Kaus wrote, "Let's see. Conservatives are for McCain. Liberals like McCain. Centrists love McCain. Doesn't that mean McCain might . . . win? Who's going to vote against him? In a general election, it seems like McCain would come close to being elected by acclamation!"[85] "Many Democrats, including some close to all the leading presidential candidates, believe that a healthy, steady McCain—if nominated by his party— would be unbeatable, no matter who the Democrats picked," said ABCNews.com's "The Note." "With those caveats about McCain, that seems like a sensible view to us."[86] Even as McCain's presidential campaign proved inept in the first half of 2007, the fundamentals of McCain's coverage—the praise of his character, the perpetuation of the Myth of McCain—were not altered.

Will the Free Ride Come to an End?

There may be no greater influence on the coverage a presidential candidate receives than what kind of guy reporters think he is. Whether they agree with his policy positions, whether he has a record of legislative accomplishment, whether his ideas for new programs are clever or ridiculous—all these factors pale in comparison to whether the reporters simply like hanging out with him. Particularly when one considers how miserable life on the campaign trail can be for a reporter—separation from family, constant deadlines, and a succession of dingy hotel rooms, bad meals, and early wake-up calls—having a candidate who is fun to cover can make all the difference in the world.

And no candidate is more fun to cover than John McCain, for reasons we have already discussed at length. Many of those reasons come down to the fact that McCain treats reporters the way they want to be treated. Not only is John McCain good with reporters, he's good *to* them as well. He stays on the record, he offers them colorful quotes, he creates a jovial atmosphere, and perhaps most of all, he seems to genuinely enjoy their company. Given the fact that most politicians treat reporters with a combination of suspicion and contempt, and endeavor to make their jobs as difficult as possible, it is hard to overstate just how much goodwill McCain's attitude has produced.

Though he had been laying its foundation for much of his career to that point, the Myth of McCain flowered fully during the 2000 presidential primaries. What is so remarkable about the press's adulation for John McCain is that it wasn't confined to the 2000 campaign; it persisted virtually unchanged in the ensuing years. While most failed presidential candidates fade away, scorned by the reporters who once looked on them as figures of national importance, McCain's stature has only grown.

Although reporters' embrace of McCain in 1999 and 2000 may have been unusual in degree, it was not unusual in kind. "In every campaign the press picks a favorite, someone they like," said Deborah Orin of the *New York Post* in 2000. "It's not done consciously. And it's probably wrong, but it happens. Reporters don't treat candidates equally."[87] In fact, in many presidential primary campaigns, the press chooses a dark-horse straight talker to whom it can give fawning, if sporadic, coverage. The stories about candidates like Mo Udall, Bruce Babbitt, or Paul Tsongas usually stress their refreshing candor and their slim chances of capturing the nomination. This kind of coverage becomes a surrogate for an attack on the nomination process itself and the demands of media-driven politics in general. The candidate who announces his intention to raise taxes (as Babbitt did) or takes some other politically dangerous position is lauded for his courage even as his campaign is framed as a quixotic, doomed effort.

The difference with McCain was that reporters didn't abandon him when his chances of winning became real. In their navel-gazing moments, reporters are often heard to say, as Gloria Borger of CBS did in September 2006, "We take people to the top of the mountain and then once we get them to the top of the mountain, it's our job to knock them down."[88] But the press never sought to knock McCain down. Even as he modified his own "straight talk" to navigate tricky political waters, they maintained their admiration. And as he launched a second run, even as he changed his position on important issues, pandered to groups he had criticized, and set about methodically to become the candidate of the "establishment" he had claimed to be fighting eight years before ("Remember, all the establishment is against us," he said in February 2000. "This is an insurgency campaign. I'm just like Luke Skywalker trying to get out of the Death Star"[89]), reporters remained loyal fans.

And even as the 2008 McCain campaign turned out, in at least its initial incarnation, to have trouble garnering substantial primary support, reporters' yearning for the days of the Straight Talk Express was evident. When McCain got back on the bus, they voiced their thanks. "Aboard the Straight Talk Express, McCain is able to recapture some of the happy-warrior magic of his insurgent odyssey of 2000," wrote Mike Allen of the *Politico*.[90] "As he toured crucial states this week after announcing his candidacy for president, Mr. McCain, a Republican of Arizona, made it clear that the policy he adopted as a candidate in 2000 of speaking freely, frequently, and at length to reporters and audiences was still in place as he struggled to regain front-runner status," wrote the *New York Times*. "For a generation of political reporters in an age when direct access even to local candidates can be rare and tightly restricted, it brought to mind an earlier era, along with questions about whether he could recapture some of the spontaneity and energy of the last campaign."[91] The affection for the Straight Talk Express, and the hope that it would return, was hard not to see.

Nonetheless, McCain's chances of becoming president looked far worse in mid-2007 than they had a year before. His ham-handed efforts to become the "establishment" candidate were unsuccessful, his advocacy of immigration reform led to displeasure among a limited but vocal portion of the Republican electorate, and his attempts to court the Christian Right could not overcome the distrust sown by his confrontation with Robertson and Falwell in 2000. But even as journalists reported on his campaign's problems, their fundamental affection for McCain remained undiminished. His integrity was a given, his nobility lauded, his character unblemished. The political process—the need to fund-raise and pander—may have taken a toll, but the man as presented was as admirable as ever. John McCain was, and is, still judged by a different standard. The Myth of McCain lives on.

For years, analysts have decried "pack journalism," the tendency of reporters to think alike, adopt the same perspectives, and chase the same stories. Nowhere is this problem more acute than on the presidential campaign trail, where reporters literally move in a pack. They ride the same bus or plane, stay in the same hotel, walk along together from event to event, and spend the bulk of their day confined to each other's company. In that atmosphere, breaking away from the conventional wisdom becomes all but impossible. Little premium is put on adopting a new outlook or questioning whether other reporters have misunderstood something fundamental about the candidate they are covering.

But let us imagine for a moment what would happen if one reporter following McCain stood up and said to his or her colleagues, "You know what? I think we've gotten McCain wrong all these years. He's not such a straight talker—sure, he's fun to shoot the breeze with, but when it comes to policy and substance he's just as full of it as any other politician. And yeah, he breaks with other Republicans now and again, but on all the important issues he votes the conservative line. So why do we keep repeating what a 'maverick' he is? Do we even ask anymore whether that's true, or do we just take it for granted? And we've seen him change positions on issues and suck up to people he has condemned in the past, so why do we forgive him for it when we wouldn't do the same for a different candidate?

"We're all impressed with what he did forty years ago in Vietnam, but after all, it was forty years ago. Wouldn't it be better to · judge his character on what he's done recently? And given how much he and his aides bring up Vietnam, isn't it time we stopped saying that he's too modest and full of integrity to use it for political advantage?

"We all know how hard he works to win our favor and how carefully he's planned how to become reporters' friend—but we still fall for it. Is he really different, or is his media strategy just better designed and executed than those of the other candidates? Why do we always give him the benefit of the doubt? Why is it that with every other candidate, we're as cynical as can be, always assuming they have bad motives, that everything they do is just for crass political gain, but with McCain we always assume his motives are pure?

"Why do we say that other candidates are adopting a persona, but McCain is just being real? Should he really be treated so differently? Don't we have an obligation to judge him by the same standards we use to judge any candidate? If we don't, aren't we doing the public a disservice?"

Given what most of the press seems to believe about John McCain, it would take a truly courageous reporter to begin asking those questions. It would take someone willing to buck the prevailing wisdom and risk the condemnation of his or her peers. It would take someone who puts principle over the immediate professional gain that goes with following the pack. It would take someone of integrity, someone who values independence. One might even say the reporter who was willing to ask those questions would be a maverick.

Postscript

As this book went to press, the news media's affection for John McCain, and all the themes and story lines that make up the Myth of McCain, were thrust once again onto the front pages and over the airwaves. After a period during which the possibility of him winning the Republican presidential nomination seemed to disappear—a decline much lamented by reporters and pundits—McCain came roaring back, propelled as always by the kind of press coverage only he receives. Though other candidates took the spotlight in the months before, once the actual primary voting approached, journalists turned their eyes back to the one who had captivated them for so long. When they did, the flavor of their coverage was much the same as it had been in the 2000 campaign, and in all the years since.

In presidential primaries, nothing matters more than "expectations." Journalists set almost arbitrary benchmarks each candidate must meet to be considered successful, then declare them winners or losers based on those standards. But as in so many areas, the ordinary rules don't seem to apply to John McCain. Before the 2008 Iowa caucus, commentators gave McCain as low a bar as one could imagine. "The big story could be if McCain comes in a respectable third," said Linda Douglass of the *National Journal.* Chris Matthews predicted McCain would win 18 percent, and said such a showing would make McCain "a big hero."[1] "Anything north of 15 percent Thursday will get played up big by the media and lead to front-runner coverage once he sets foot in New Hampshire again," wrote Chuck Todd, the political director of NBC News.[2]

It was left to Matthews, as usual the most starry-eyed of McCain's media fans, to wax poetic. "Ladies and gentlemen, there's something real here, courage to endure repeated disappointment, unexpected failure, shattering defeat," he said on *Hardball* the night before the caucus. "That's what people respected in Britain's Winston Churchill, and it's so much who John McCain is this second and final run for the presidency. There's something genuine here, something selfless, even quietly grand in his campaign."[3]

But Todd realized what was beginning to happen. "You know, I hate to be existential here, but you know, the media—and I say this as if I'm not a member of it—but the media does seem to be ready to will John McCain out of Iowa," he said in response to Matthews. "It is a stunning thing. And if I were Mitt Romney or Giuliani or Mike Huckabee, I'd be like, 'Wait a minute! You're going to take a third place finish and somehow use that to catapult this guy, [give him] free media, and get him the victory in New

Hampshire?' But frankly, that is what's going to happen. There's a reason John McCain is sort of the king of sort of working the media."[4]

Todd did get one thing wrong: McCain ended up coming in fourth in Iowa, not third. And he only received 13 percent of the vote, less than what had been predicted. So how did the press react?

By declaring him the victor. "This is a fantastic night for John McCain," said Mike Allen of the *Politico*.[5] "This could not have been conceivably a better result for McCain," said Fred Barnes on Fox News.[6] "This is very good news for John McCain," declared Tom Brokaw.[7] Ignoring the Republicans who came in first, second, and third in Iowa, Tim Russert immediately booked McCain for a coveted interview on that Sunday's *Meet the Press*.

When McCain won the New Hampshire primary the following Tuesday, commentators did not simply offer praise. Instead, they talked about the victory as though it were somehow a realization of electoral justice, the true John McCain returning and being rightly rewarded by the voters. Jon Meacham, the editor of *Newsweek*, went on the air to echo what he had written a week before: "The apparent reconsideration of the candidacy of John McCain is good news for all of us, whatever our politics, for McCain has proved in the campaign what he proved in Vietnam: that patience is a virtue, and, when in doubt, principle is worth a try."[8] Like many candidates before him (John Kerry, four years earlier, to take just one example), McCain's campaign went through a low period, but the candidate continued to campaign. What did Tom Brokaw see in this persistence? Nothing less than heroism, and echoes of McCain the prisoner of war. "His staff, his longest serving staff, his closest friends left. The campaign was in deep financial difficulty. And John McCain got on the trail with Cindy, on his own again. And it does remind you, as I've said here before, this is a guy who spent five and a half years being tortured almost every day." Chris Matthews agreed, saying that continuing to campaign demonstrated "a special kind of courage."[9]

On CNN, Gloria Borger closed the circle of the argument the press had made back when McCain was larding his campaign with lobbyists and genuflecting before religious extremists. That earlier McCain was a momentary lapse, but the real and virtuous McCain had returned: "He was the establishment candidate. That didn't work for him," Borger said, "so after July when he was broke and he had to fire most of his staff, he said, I'm going to go back to being John McCain. I'm going to go back to New Hampshire and work those town halls and be who I am, and I'm going to become the maverick Republican again."[10]

The "real" McCain was back, and the reporters back on board the Straight Talk Express couldn't have sounded happier. "It has been tough to avoid a sense this week that some of the coverage has been shaped by journalists rooting for certain outcomes," wrote John Harris and Jim VandeHei in the *Politico* after New Hampshire. "Many journalists are enamored with McCain because of the access he gives and, above all, the belief that he is free of political artifice."[11]

Just as it had so many times before, John McCain's carefully considered and deftly executed press management strategy had its desired effect: admiring journalists, trying without much success to hold their feelings in check as they penned report after glowing report about the straight-talking maverick riding a wave of righteousness and truth over the American political landscape. It sounded just like old times.

—JANUARY 14, 2008

Notes

Foreword

1   Michael Barone, ed., *The Almanac of American Politics 2006*. Washington, D.C.: National Journal Group, 2006, p. 94.

2   R. W. Apple Jr., "A Beginning, Not an End," *New York Times*, February 2, 2000, p. A1.

3   Jacob Weisberg, "Super Tuesday: Instant Analysis," *Slate*, March 7, 2000.

4   Alison Mitchell, "Underdog McCain Develops Anti-Campaign Style," *New York Times*, December 12, 1999, p. 42.

5   Howard Kurtz, "Nothing Succeeds Like Access," *Washington Post*, December 8, 1999, p. C1.

6   David Nyhan, "McCain's Ace in the Hole," *Boston Globe*, July 2, 1999, p. A19.

7   Roger Simon, "Honest John, on the Loose," *U.S. News & World Report*, September 27, 1999, p. 26.

8   Mike Wallace, quoted in Howard Kurtz, "A Running Start? Sen. John McCain, the Media's Man of the Hour," *Washington Post*, June 8, 1998, p. D1.

9   This quote appeared in Pat Murphy, "Free Ride," *In These Times*, March 2000.

10 Michael Lewis, "A Question of Honor," *New York Times Magazine*, May 25, 1997, p. 32.

11 Joe Klein, *Politics Lost: How American Democracy Was Trivialized by People Who Think You're Stupid*. New York: Doubleday, 2006, p. 159.

12 David Broder, "Straight Talking Again," *Washington Post*, April 27, 2007, p. A23.

13 Editorial, "Reality Show," *Washington Post*, April 29, 2007, p. B6.

14 Evan Thomas, "The Truman Primary," *Newsweek*, May 14, 2007, p. 24.

15 *Nightline*, ABC, March 26, 2007.

Chapter 1

1 "This is classic John McCain, the anti-candidate." Linda Feldmann, "McCain Plays the Role of Maverick in 2000 Race," *Christian Science Monitor*, August 10, 1999, p. 2. See also, for example, Richard Reeves, "The Anti-Candidate," Universal Press Syndicate, February 16, 2000.

2 "In short, if Bill Clinton was the master politician who transformed strategists like James Carville into cult figures and brought campaign stagecraft to a new high gloss, then Mr. McCain is running as the blunt anti-politician who won't lie, who won't spin." Allison Mitchell, "Underdog McCain Develops Anti-Campaign Style," *New York Times*, December 12, 1999, p. A42.

3 Mary Jacoby, "McCain Stays a Pesky Thorn in Bush's Side," *St. Petersburg Times*, February 18, 2001, p. 1A.

4 John Hughes, "Gas Prices and Iraq Shroud Predictions of Next US President," *Christian Science Monitor*, May 24, 2006.

5 Steve Bousquet, "McCain Backs Crist in Governor's Race," *St. Petersburg Times*, August 8, 2006, p. 5A.

6 Mary Orndorff, "Earlier Primary Brings Attention," *Birmingham News*, September 14, 2006, p. A1.

7 Ralph Z. Hallow, "This Senator Bends, but He Never Breaks," *Washington Times*, May 26, 1998, p. A1.

8 "White House Avoids McCain-Hastert Dispute," Associated Press, May 20, 2004.

9 Tony Batt, "Arizona Senator Seeks to Reintroduce Bill Banning Wagers on Collegiate Sports," *Las Vegas Review Journal*, April 9, 2003.

10 Gerald Shields, "McCain's Already Running in Louisiana," *Advocate* (Baton Bouge, LA), August 20, 2006, p. B13.

11 "McCain Postpones Decision on Treatment," *Chicago Tribune*, August 18, 2000, p. C2.

12 "Pumping Iron, Digging Gold, Pressing Flesh," *Newsweek*, November 20, 2000, p. 50.

13 *World News*, ABC, May 17, 2006.

14 These figures were obtained by searching LexisNexis for "McCain and Vietnam and prisoner of war." As such, they probably understate the frequency of such mentions, because some articles will reference McCain's captivity without using the phrase "prisoner of war."

15 E. J. Montini, "Dousing Senator Hothead," *Arizona Republic*, November 7, 1999, p. 1B.

16 Charles P. Pierce, "John McCain Walks on Water," *Esquire*, May 1, 1998.

17 Todd Purdum, "McCain Joins Campaign Fray, Displaying Independent Streak," *New York Times*, March 19, 2004, p. A1.

18 Howard Kurtz, "Nothing Succeeds Like Access; Does John McCain Have the Media Eating out of His Hand?" *Washington Post*, December 8, 1999, p. C1.

19 E. J. Montini, "McCain's Grave Concern," *Arizona Republic*, November 21, 1999, p. 1B.

20 Bill Muller, "The Life Story of Arizona's Maverick Senator McCain," *Arizona Republic*, October 3, 1999, p. 3M.

21 *Meet the Press*, NBC, April 2, 2006.

22 Jerry Kammer, "Hail to the Champs," *Arizona Republic*, December 14, 2001, p. C1.

23 *Larry King Live*, CNN, November 15, 1999.

24 Amy Silverman, "Dear John," *Phoenix New Times*, July 2, 1998.

25 Michael Kranish, "Dole Is Reported to Cut Running Mate List to 3," *Boston Globe*, August 8, 1996, p. A28.

26 Bill Muller, "The Life Story of Arizona's Maverick Senator McCain," *Arizona Republic*, October 3, 1999, p. 3M.

27 Bill Sammon, "Meet the Next President: McCain the Maverick," *Washington Examiner*, September 15, 2006.

28 Howard Kurtz, "A Running Start," *Washington Post*, June 8, 1998, p. D1.

29 Chris Jones, "One of Us," *Esquire*, August 2006.

30 David Plotz, "Sen. John McCain," *Slate*, June 28, 1998.

31 Matt Labash, "Lobbyists for McCain," *Weekly Standard*, February 21, 2000, p. 15.

32 May 20, 2006, www.huffingtonpost.com/2006/05/21/top-mccain-aide-insults-e_n_21405.html.

33 Joe Conason, "Say It Ain't So, John," *Salon*, July 8, 2004.

34 David Grann, "The Hero Myth," *New Republic*, May 24,1999, p. 24.

35 *Hardball*, MSNBC, November 10, 2006.

36 Allan Wolper and Greg Mitchell, *Editor & Publisher*, January 31, 2000, p. 18.

37 Amy Silverman, "The Pampered Politician," *Phoenix New Times*, May 15, 1997.

38 During those years the *Post* wrote 177 editorials on campaign finance reform, and the *Times* wrote 165.

39 James Warren, "Senator Launches Novel Campaign Against Money Politics," *Chicago Tribune*, June 27, 1999, p. C2.

40 *CBS This Morning*, CBS, September 27, 1999.

41 References to "Feingold-McCain" appeared until around the end of 1998.

42 For instance, a July 2000 CBS News poll asked, "Currently parties are able to raise unlimited amounts of money from individuals and organizations to spend on issue ads during political campaigns—called soft money. Do you think these types of contributions should be allowed, or do you think they should be banned?" Only 25 percent said soft money should be allowed, while 64 percent said it should be banned.

43 Editorial, "An Extraordinary Victory," *New York Times*, March 21, 2002, p. A36.

44 Editorial, "Victory for Reform, *Washington Post*, Match 21, 2002, p. A34.

45 Editorial, "Armageddon for the GOP? Hardly." *Wall Street Journal*, February 20, 2002.

46 Seth Gitell, "The Democratic Party Suicide Bill," *Atlantic Monthly*, July 1, 2003, p. 106.

47 Holly Ramer, "Conservative Group's Ad Blasts McCain," Associated Press, December 23, 1999.

48 *The Beltway Boys*, Fox News, March 30, 2002.

49 NBC/*Wall Street Journal* poll, April 2001.

50 Andrew Ferguson, "McCain's Fans Fight Disillusionment," Bloomberg News, April 25, 2006.

51 *Hardball*, MSNBC, September 29, 2004.

52 Bush's suits may actually cost much more; he buys from Oxxford Clothes, the most elite tailor in the United States. According to the *Chicago Tribune*, "Oxxford produces only 30,000 units a year, and off-the-rack suits range from $1,900 to $2,750. Add about 12 percent to the price for made to measure. Oxxford also offers custom suits beginning at $3,000 through Bergdorf Goodman in New York and Louis, Boston in Boston." (James L. Johnson, "Impeccable Fit," *Chicago Tribune*, September 12, 1999, p. C19.) The Scottish newspaper the *Express* reported in 2002, "American leader George W. Bush personally picked out a plain navy blue wool woven by the small family firm of Reid & Taylor in the Borders . . . Mr. Crittenden Rawlings, of Chicago tailors Oxxford Clothes, was with President Bush when he was selecting the fabric for his suits. He said: 'The president chooses all his own clothes. He chose about 10 pieces of fabric from the selection.'" "Borders Firm Provides Cloth for Presidential Wardrobe," *Express*, October 24, 2002, p. 9.

53 *Special Report with Brit Hume*, Fox News, July 3, 2004.

54 Andrew Ferguson, "The Media's Favorite Republican," *Weekly Standard*, July 6, 1998, p. 20.

55 Allan Wolper and Greg Mitchell, *Editor & Publisher*, January 31, 2000, p. 18.

56 David Nyhan, "Relentless Reformer," *Boston Globe*, November 14, 1997, p. A25.

57 Tish Durkin, "The Twisted Relationship Between John McCain and the Press," *National Journal*, June 9, 2001, pp. 1699–1700.

58 Bill Minutaglio, *First Son: George W. Bush and the Bush Family Dynasty*. New York: Three Rivers Press, 2001, p. 223.

59 Ken Auletta, "Fortress Bush," *New Yorker*, January 19, 2004, p. 53.

60 Amy Silverman, "The Pampered Politician," *Phoenix New Times*, May 15, 1997.

61 Dick Polman, "Welcome to McCain's Flip-Flop Express," *Philadelphia Inquirer*, February 18, 2007, p. E1.

62 Mark Halperin and John Harris, *The Way to Win: Taking the White House in 2008*. New York: Random House, 2006, p. 180.

63 Judging from news reports, the bus seems to have been given the moniker sometime in the summer of 1999.

64 Tucker Carlson, *Politicians, Partisans, and Parasites: My Adventures in Cable News*. New York: Warner Books, 2003, pp. 112–113.

65 Roger Simon, "Honest John, on the Loose," *U.S. News and World Report*, September 27, 1999, p. 26.

66 Joe Klein, *Politics Lost: How American Democracy Was Trivialized by People Who Think You're Stupid*. New York: Doubleday, 2006, p. 166.

67 David Foster Wallace, *Consider the Lobster and Other Essays*. New York: Little, Brown, 2006, p. 214–215.

68 Jeff Fishel, *Presidents and Promises: From Campaign Pledge to Presidential Performance*. Washington, DC: CQ Press, 1985. See also Kathleen Hall Jamieson, *Everything You Think You Know About Politics and Why You're Wrong*. New York: Basic Books, 2000.

69 Matt Welch, "Do We Need Another T.R.?" *Los Angeles Times*, November 26, 2006, p. M1.

Chapter 2

1 Robert Timberg, *John McCain: An American Odyssey*. New York: Touchstone, 1999.

2 ibid.

3 ibid., p. 131.

4 ibid., pp. 124–125.

5 Robert Timberg, *A Nightingale's Song*. New York: Touchstone, 1995, p. 139.

6 ibid., p. 140.

7 ibid., p. 143.

8 Jill Zuckman, "McCain's Book Breaks Silence on Ordeal," *Boston Globe*, September 12, 1999, p. A8.

9 Bill Muller, "The Life Story of Arizona's Maverick Senator McCain," *Arizona Republic*, October 3, 1999, p. 3M.

10 Chris Suellentrop, "Is John McCain a Crook?" *Slate*, February 18, 2000.

11 Margaret Carlson, "Seven Sorry Senators," *Time*, January 8, 1990, p. 48.

12 Charles Lewis and the Center for Public Integrity, *The Buying of the President 2000*. New York: Avon Books, 2000, p. 286.

13 Bill Muller, "The Life Story of Arizona's Maverick Senator McCain," *Arizona Republic*, October 3, 1999, p. 3M.

14 ibid.

15 ibid.

16 Charles R. Babcock, "5 Senators and a Failed S&L," *Washington Post*, November 19, 1989, p. A1.

17 Douglas Franz, "The 2000 Campaign: The Arizona Ties: A Beer Baron and a Powerful Publisher Put McCain on a Political Path," *New York Times*, February 21, 2000, p. A14.

18 Charles R. Babcock, "5 Senators and a Failed S&L," *Washington Post*, November 19, 1989, p. A1.

19 Glenn R. Simpson, "Activist Who Headed Mecham Recall Drive Is Faltering Against McCain and DeConcini," *Roll Call*, February 15, 1990.

20 Chris Suellentrop, "Is John McCain a Crook?" *Slate*, February 18, 2000.

21 "The Keating Five: Still Stinking," *Economist*, March 9, 1991, p. 27.

22 Walter V. Robinson, "Campaign 2000: Pluck, Leaks Helped Senator to Overcome S&L Scandal," *Boston Globe*, February 29, 2000, p. A1.

23 ibid.

24 ibid.

25 ibid.

26 Although some estimates of the total cost of the scandal range as high as $500 billion, direct costs to the federal government were probably closer to $125 billion. See Timothy Curry and Lynn Shibut, "The Cost of the Savings and Loan Crisis: Truth and Consequences," *FDIC Banking Review*, December 2000, pp. 26–35.

27 Bill Muller, "Chapter V: The Keating Five," *Arizona Republic*, October 3, 1999.

28 ibid.

29 Charles R. Babcock, "5 Senators and a Failed S&L," *Washington Post*, November 19, 1989, p. A1.

30 Bill Muller, "The Life Story of Arizona's Maverick Senator McCain," *Arizona Republic*, October 3, 1999, p. 3M.

31 Peter Robinson, "Worth the Fighting For: A Conversation with John McCain," *Uncommon Knowledge*, Hoover Institution, November 7, 2002, www.hoover.org/publications/uk/2995746.html.

32 Bill Muller, "The Life Story of Arizona's Maverick Senator McCain," *Arizona Republic*, October 3, 1999, p. 3M.

33 Rich Lowry, "The Allure of John McCain," *National Review*, September 27, 1999, p. 36.

34 Amy Silverman, "The Pampered Politician: Arizona Senator John McCain Is Ready for a Presidential Run—if the National Press Corps Has Anything to Say About It," *Phoenix New Times*, May 15, 1997.

35 This search excluded some instances in which a letter to the editor mentioned the Keating Five.

36 Nancy Gibbs and John F. Dickerson, "The Power and the Story," *Time*, December 13, 1999, p. 40.

37 Connie Bruck, "McCain's Party," *New Yorker*, May 30, 2005, p. 15.

38 Nancy Gibbs and John F. Dickerson, "The Power and the Story," *Time*, December 13, 1999, p. 40.

39 Jack Anderson and Jan Moller, "McCain Learned His Lessons from Keating Scandal," United Features Syndicate, January 3, 1999.

40 Sean Mussenden, "Budget Hawk Will Weight Space Program," *Orlando Sentinel*, February 10, 2003, p. A9.

41 Debra Saunders, "Who's the Monkey Now?" *San Francisco Chronicle*, November 22, 2005, p. B7.

42 *Hardball*, MSNBC, August 30, 2004.

43 Steven V. Roberts, "House, 270–161, Votes to Invoke War Powers Act," *New York Times*, September 29, 1983, p. A1.

44 Kirk Victor, "McCain's Evolution," *National Journal*, August 8, 2001, p. 2464.

45 Julia Anderson, States News Service, February 16, 1989.

46 Stephanie Saul, "Senate Showdown to Begin on F-14D," *Newsday*, July 13, 1989, p. 2.

47 Ellen Gamerman, "McCain Leaves His Mark on Campaign Finance Bill," States News Service, June 8, 1993.

48 Helen Dewar, "Campaign Finance Bill Seen Gaining in Senate," *Washington Post*, May 30, 1993, p. A4.

49 Helen Dewar, "Senate's Republican Moderates," *Washington Post*, July 29, 1993, p. A7.

50 Larry Margasak, "Clinton Prods Key Republicans as Campaign Finance Debate Drags On," Associated Press, June 15, 1993.

51 Tim Curran, "House Says Senate Reform Bill D.O.A," *Roll Call*, June 21, 1993.

52 James Kitfield, "The Maverick," *National Journal*, November 25, 1995, p. 2923.

53 ibid.

54 ibid.

55 William Safire, "San Diego Speech Scorecard," *New York Times*, August 19, 1996, p. A13.

56 "Time's 25 Most Influential Americans: John McCain, U.S. Senator, Arizona," *Time*, April 21, 1997, p. 40.

57 S 1414. thomas.loc.gov/cgi-bin/bdquery/z?d105:SN01415:@@@L&summ2 =m&>.

58 Maureen Dowd, "No More Wagging," *New York Times*, January 3, 1999, p. 9.

59 Charlie Cook, "Enough Already! Stop the Slobbering," *National Journal*, May 13, 2000, p. 1548.

60 Stuart Rothenberg, "Reputation as Maverick Could Benefit McCain in 2000 Presidential Bid," *Roll Call*, January 14, 1999.

61 Scott Lindlaw, "Senator Plots Presidential Strategy," Associated Press, January 18, 1999.

62 Margaret Carlson, "All Quiet on the Insider Front," *Time*, February 1, 1999, p. 30.

63 Mary McGrory, "Friendly Fire," *Washington Post*, May 20, 1999, p. A3.

64 William Safire, "Independents' Day," *New York Times*, July 5, 1999, p. A11.

65 It should be noted that CNN makes a wider range of its programming available on the Nexis database, raising the possibility of skewed results. However, most of the results of our search were in time slots during which competing cable news networks also provided transcripts to Nexis.

66 *Inside Politics*, CNN, April 2, 1999.

67 *Late Edition with Wolf Blitzer*, CNN, August 22, 1999.

68 *The World Today*, CNN, September 27, 1999.

69 *Inside Politics*, CNN, November 22, 1999.

70 *Crossfire*, CNN, December 6, 1999.

71 Alison Mitchell, "Anti-Politician McCain Shows Political Skills," *New York Times*, December 30, 1999, p. A1.

72 Poll, *Washington Post*, June 5–6, 1999, www.pollingreport.com/wh2rep.htm.

73 "Today's National Polls," *National Journal* Poll Track, February 29, 2000.

74 David C. Barker and Adam B. Lawrence, "Media Favoritism and Presidential Nominations: Reviving the Direct Effects Model," *Political Communication* 23:41–59 (2006).

75 E. R. Shipp, "Typecasting Candidates," *Washington Post*, March 5, 2000, p. B6.

76 *Hardball*, MSNBC, June 21, 2006.

77 Mickey Kaus, "Gore's Press Problem," *Slate*, January 31, 2000.

78 Ramesh Ponnuru, "McCainiacs," *National Review*, March 20, 2000, p. 17.

79 Jacob Weisberg, "Super Tuesday: Instant Analysis," *Slate*, March 7, 2000.

80 Jonathan Alter, "The Politics of Personality," *Newsweek*, March 6, 2000, p. 34.

81 David Grann, "Race Against Himself," *New Republic*, March 13, 2000, p. 32.

82 ibid.

83 *CBS News Special Report*, CBS, December 13, 2000.

84 *Inside Politics*, CNN, January 4, 2001.

85 David Corn, "McCain in Vain?" *Nation*, June 25, 2001, p. 5.

86 Allison Mitchell, "Foes of Abortion Split Sharply over Campaign Finance Bill," *New York Times*, March 26, 1998, p. A21.

87 "Even if he somehow extricates himself from those positions, McCain would not have an easy time explaining why he nominated Bush as a 2001 'Man of the Year' in the conservative publication *Human Events*. And after that, he would have to explain to Democrats one more thing: why he reads *Human Events*." Charles Mahtesian, "There's No Getting Past His Past," *National Journal*, May 1, 2004, p. 1350.

88 Ramesh Ponnuru, "McCainiacs," *National Review*, March 20, 2000, p. 17.

89 John Heilemann, "N.Y.'s Favorite Republicans," *New York*, December 19, 2000, p. 22.

90 See Philip Paolino and Daron Shaw, "Lifting the Hood on the Straight-Talk Express: Examining the McCain Phenomenon," *American Politics Research* 29(5), September 2001, pp. 483–506.

91 Grover Norquist, "Mopping Up After McCain," *American Spectator*, May 2000, p. 70.

92 John Judis, "Razing McCain," *American Prospect*, March 13, 2000, p. 15.

93 "Citizen McCain," editorial, *New York Times*, March 21, 2004, p. 10.

94 Mark Leibovich, "Pedal to the Metal," *Washington Post*, May 12, 2004, p. C1.

95 David Broder, "The McCain Phenomenon," *Washington Post*, August 31, 2004, p. A21.

96 Melinda Henneberger, "The Man in the Middle," *Newsweek*, September 6, 2004, p. 30.

97 Dana Milbank, "McCain Honored for Tackles as a Team Player," *Washington Post*, September 26, 2004, p. A4.

98 *Fox News Watch*, Fox News, May 1, 2004.

99 Eric Boehlert, "The Press vs. Al Gore," *Rolling Stone*, December 6–13, 2001.

Chapter 3

1 E. J. Montini, "Arizona's Prince Charming," *Arizona Republic*, December 7, 1999, p. 1B.

2 ibid.

3 Bill Muller, "The Life Story of Arizona's Maverick Senator McCain," *Arizona Republic*, October 3, 1999, p. 3M.

4 "Best and Worst of Congress '06," *Washingtonian*, September 2006.

5 Gallup Poll, August 9, 2006.

6 Harry Jaffe, "Senator Hothead," *Washingtonian*, February 1997, p. 64.

7 Pat Murphy, "Free Ride," *In These Times*, March 2000.

8 Bill Muller, "The Life Story of Arizona's Maverick Senator McCain," *Arizona Republic*, October 3, 1999, p. 3M.

9 Amy Silverman, "Don't Cross John McCain," *Playboy*, February 2000, p. 118.

10 Kris Mayes and Charles Kelly, "Stories Surface on Senator's Demeanor," *Arizona Republic*, November 5, 1999, p. 1A.

11 Amy Silverman, "Don't Cross John McCain," *Playboy*, February 2000, p. 118.

12 Bill Muller, "The Life Story of Arizona's Maverick Senator McCain," *Arizona Republic*, October 3, 1999, p. 3M.

13 David Grann, "The Hero Myth," *New Republic*, May 24, 1999, p. 24.

14 The *New Times* interviewed McCain on this topic in 1994; the quote appears in Amy Silverman, "The Pampered Politician," *Phoenix New Times*, May 15, 1997.

15 David Broder, "For McCain, No Place Like Home for Controversy," *Washington Post*, November 28, 1999, p. A1.

16 Amy Silverman, "Statesman or Henchman?", *Phoenix New Times*, March 23, 1994, www.phoenixnewtimes.com/Issues/1994-03-23/news/feature3.html.

17 David Broder, "For McCain, No Place Like Home for Controversy," *Washington Post*, November 28, 1999, p. A1.

18 Amy Silverman, "Statesman or Henchman?", *Phoenix New Times*, March 23, 1994, www.phoenixnewtimes.com/Issues/1994-03-23/news/feature3.html.

19 Frank Bruni, "Arizona Governor Expected to Endorse Bush Over State's 2 Favorite Sons," *New York Times*, September 25, 1999, p. A10.

20 Richard L. Berke, "McCain Having to Prove Himself Even in Arizona," *New York Times*, October 25, 1999, p. A1.

21 David Broder, "For McCain, No Place Like Home for Controversy," *Washington Post*, November 28, 1999, p. A1.

22 Norman Ornstein, "Minority Report," *Atlantic Monthly*, December 1985, p. 30.

23 Charles Fenyvesi, "Washington Whispers," *U.S. News & World Report*, March 13, 1989, p. 17.

24 John F. Dickerson, "In This Corner . . . ," *Time*, November 15, 1999, p. 38.

25 John W. Mashek, "For Sen. Kennedy, a Day of Sympathy and Anger," *Boston Globe*, August 6, 1993, p. 14.

26 Ronald Kessler, "McCain's Out-of-Control Anger," NewsMax, July 5, 2006.

27 Jake Tapper, "How Tough Is John McCain?" *Salon*, May 14, 1999.

28 Evan Thomas, "Senator Hothead," *Newsweek*, February 21, 2000, p. 24.

29 John F. Dickerson, "In This Corner . . . ," *Time*, November 15, 1999, p. 38.

30 Kris Mayes and Charles Kelly, "Stories Surface on Senator's Demeanor," *Arizona Republic*, November 5, 1999, p. 1A.

31 Walter V. Robinson, "In Arizona, McCain's Tactics Seen as Power Plays," *Boston Globe*, December 13, 1999, p. A1.

32 ibid.

33 Pat Murphy, "Free Ride," *In These Times*, March 2000.

34 Amy Silverman, "Don't Cross John McCain," *Playboy*, February 2000, p. 118.

35 Allan Wolper and Greg Mitchell, *Editor & Publisher*, January 31, 2000, p. 18.

36 Adrianne Flynn, "My Life with Candor Man," *American Journalism Review*, April 2000, p. 18.

37 Allan Wolper and Greg Mitchell, *Editor & Publisher*, January 31, 2000, p. 18.

38 Editorial, "McCain's Temper Is Legitimate Issue," *Arizona Republic*, October 31, 1999, p. 6B.

39 Scott Thomsen, "McCain's Temper May Become an Issue," Associated Press, October 31, 1999.

40 Thomas Vinciguerra, "Word for Word: Chief Executive Anger," *New York Times*, November 7, 1999, "Week in Review," p. 7.

41 Lars-Erik Nelson, "McCain Gets Mad? So What?" *Daily News* (New York), November 3, 1999, p. 43.

42 "Viewpoint," *Editor & Publisher*, November 6, 1999, p. 14.

43 Walter V. Robinson, "In Arizona, McCain's Tactics Seen as Power Plays," *Boston Globe*, December 13, 1999, p. A1.

44 David Plotz, "Sen. John McCain: The Media Want Him to Be President. It's a Bad Idea" (sidebar), *Slate*, June 28, 1998.

45 "McCain's Temper May Become an Issue," Associated Press, October 31, 1999.

46 Editorial, "McCain's Temper Is Legitimate Issue," *Arizona Republic*, October 31, 1999, p. 6B.

47 Richard L. Berke, "McCain Having to Prove Himself Even in Arizona," *New York Times*, October 25, 1999, p. A1.

48 Paul West, "McCain Adopts Insider Strategy," *Sun* (Baltimore), March 20, 2006, p. 1A.

49 Maureen Dowd, "The Joke's on Him," *New York Times*, June 21, 1998, p. A15.

50 David Corn, "A Joke Too Bad to Print?" *Salon*, June 25, 1998.

51 Ron Fournier, "Loose Talk Can Hurt, McCain Admits," Associated Press, September 1, 1999.

52 Joe Sciacca, "Watch What You Say in New England, George," *Boston Herald*, June 14, 1999, p. 4.

53 Ron Fournier, "Loose Talk Can Hurt, McCain Admits," Associated Press, September 1, 1999.

54 Evan Thomas, "Senator Hothead," *Newsweek*, February 21, 2000, p. 24.

55 Roger L. Simon, "Honest John, on the Loose," *U.S. News & World Report*, September 27, 1999, p. 26.

56 Ben Stocking and Maureen Fan, "McCain Says Slur Describes Captors," *Mercury News* (San Jose, CA), February 18, 2000, p. 1A.

57 Steven Thomma and Ben Stocking, "McCain Defends His Use of Anti-Viet Slur," *Miami Herald*, February 18, 2000, p. A1.

58 Frank Bruni and Alison Mitchell, "The 2000 Campaign: The Republicans: Bush and McCain Scurry Toward Showdown," *New York Times*, February 18, 2000, p. A1.

59 David Barstow, "The 2000 Campaign: Campaign Briefing," *New York Times*, February 25, 2000, p. A14.

60 Ben Stocking and Maureen Fan, "McCain Says Slur Describes Captors," *Mercury News* (San Jose, CA), February 18, 2000, p. 1A.

61 Terry Neal and Edward Walsh, "Racial Issues Dog GOP Foes," *Washington Post*, February 18, 2000, p. A6.

62 Christopher Ho, letter to the editor, *New York Times*, February 25, 2000, p. A18.

63 Andrew S. Wolfe, letter to the editor, *Washington Post*, February 24, 2000, p. A20.

64 Stephen Chapman, "John McCain Is a War Hero. So What?" *Chicago Tribune*, February 27, 2000, p. 21C.

65 "McCain Apologizes for Bigoted Language," *Asian Reporter*, March 6, 2000, p. 1.

66 Howard Kurtz, "Nothing Succeeds Like Access: Does John McCain Have the Media Eating Out of His Hand?" *Washington Post*, December 8, 1999, p. C1.

67 *Special Report with Brit Hume*, Fox News, December 8, 1999.

68 E. J. Montini, "Arizona's Prince Charming," *Arizona Republic*, December 7, 1999, p. 1B.

Chapter 4

1 Howard Kurtz, "A Running Start," *Washington Post*, June 8, 1998, p. D1.

2 Joe Crea, "Straight Talk Express Travels Down K Street," *Legal Times*, March 27, 2006, p. 18.

3 Craig Gilbert, "The Authenticity Beat," *American Journalism Review*, March 2000, p. 46.

4 This information can be found at the Center for Responsive Politics, www.opensecrets.org.

5 Michael Isikoff, "The Reformer Tunes His Money Machine," *Newsweek*, November 1, 1999, p. 40.

6 John Dunbar, Daniel Lathrop, and Robert Morlino, "Networks of Influence: The Political Power of the Communications Industry," Center for Public Integrity, October 28, 2004, www.publicintegrity.org.

7 Charles Lewis, "Media Money," *Columbia Journalism Review*, September–October 2000, p. 20.

8 Michael Isikoff, "The Reformer Tunes His Money Machine," *Newsweek*, November 1, 1999, p. 40.

9 David Willman and Anne-Marie O'Connor, "McCain Defends Letters Sent on Donors' Behalf," *Los Angeles Times*, January 9, 2000, p. 4.

10 John Mintz and Susan B. Glasser, "McCain Intervened with U.S. for 15 Campaign Contributors," *Washington Post*, January 9, 2000, p. A1.

11 "McCain: Reformer's' Backers Call Beltway Home," Center for Public Integrity, March 2, 2000, www.publicintegrity.org.

12 A LexisNexis search of all news on all available dates of "John McCain," "gaming industry," and "contributions" yields only seventy-nine results. Without

"contributions," the total goes up to three hundred. Substitute "vote" for "contributions" and the total is one hundred and nine. Those results span sixteen years of coverage, from 1990 to the present, barely a blip.

13 Amy Silverman, "Haunted by Spirits," *Phoenix New Times*, February 17, 2000.

14 Douglas Franz, "A Beer Baron and a Powerful Publisher Put McCain on a Political Path," *New York Times*, February 21, 2000, p. A14.

15 "McCain: Reformer's Backers Call Beltway Home," Center for Public Integrity, March 2, 2000, www.publicintegrity.org.

16 Chris Cilizza, "McCain Elevates Loeffler," washingtonpost.com, March 8, 2007.

17 According to the indictment, Nelson was a key conduit at the Republican National Committee in the money-laundering operation.

18 Robert Novak, "Is GOP '08 Choice Already Written in Inc.?" *Chicago Sun-Times*, December 14, 2006, p. 43.

19 Billy House and Matt Dempsey, "McCain Tapping Bush's Donors," *Arizona Republic*, December 19, 2006.

20 Wayne Slater, "Bush Accepted Twice As Many Rides Than [*sic*] McCain, Records Show," *Dallas Morning News*, February 17, 2000.

21 Evan Thomas, "Senator Hothead," *Newsweek*, February 21, 2000, p. 24.

22 Gloria Borger, "Does Barack Really Rock?" *U.S. News & World Report*, October 26, 2006, www.usnews.com/usnews/news/articles/061029/6glo.htm.

23 Richard Lowry, "The Allure of John McCain," *National Review*, September 27, 1999, p. 36.

24 Mark Murray, "Where McCain Stands," *National Journal*, February 12, 2000, p. 464.

25 Jason Horowitz, "Senator McCain Worked Blue," *New York Observer*, May 29, 2006, p. 1.

26 *Face the Nation*, CBS, January 9, 2000.

27 Mike Ferullo, "Apologetic McCain Calls for Removal of Confederate Battle Flag From S.C. Statehouse," cnn.com, April 19, 2000, archives.cnn.com/2000/ALLPOLITICS/stories/04/19/mccain.sc/.

28 *The Early Show*, CBS, October 15, 2002.

29 Editorial, "Mr. McCain's Message on Race," *New York Times*, April 21, 2000, p. A22.

30 "Confession and Confederacy," *Washington Post*, April 21, 2000, p. A26.

31 Max Blumenthal, "Beyond Macaca: The Photograph That Haunts George Allen," thenation.com, August 29, 2006.

32 "Partisan View," *Southern Partisan*, Fall 1983.

33 ibid., Winter 1989.

34 None of the thirty-nine articles in 2006 mentioning both McCain and Quinn in the LexisNexis database mentioned Quinn's background, much less critiqued McCain's hiring of him.

35   *CBS Evening News*, CBS, October 19, 2006.

36   *Today*, NBC, January 25, 2006.

37   Peter Baker, "GOP Infighting on Detainees Intensifies," *Washington Post*, September 16, 2006, p. A1.

38   Kate Zernike, "Rebuff for Bush on How to Treat Terror Suspects," *New York Times*, September 15, 2006, p. A1.

39   Editorial, "A Crucial Choice," *Washington Post*, September 14, 2006, p. A20.

40   James Gerstenzang and Noam N. Levey, "Bush Fires Back at Republican Rebels," *Los Angeles Times*, September 16, 2006, p. A14.

41   *The Situation Room*, CNN, September 14, 2006.

42   Robert J. Caldwell, "Bush, McCain, and 'Torture,'" *San Diego Union-Tribune*, September 24, 2006, p. G1.

43   Gail Russell Chaddock, "Why GOP Trio Is Bucking the White House," *Christian Science Monitor*, September 18, 2006, p. 1.

44   Kate Zernike, "Top Republicans Reach an Accord on Detainee Bill," *New York Times*, September 22, 2006, p. A1.

45   Julian E. Barnes and Richard Simon, "Bush Bows to Senators on Detainees," *Los Angeles Times*, September 22, 2006, p. A1.

46   *ABC World News with Charles Gibson*, ABC, September 21, 2006.

47   Kate Zernike, "Top Republicans Reach an Accord on Detainee Bill," *New York Times*, September 22, 2006, p. A1.

48   Marty Lederman, "Senators Snatch Defeat from Jaws of Victory: U.S. to be First Nation to Authorize Violations of Geneva," *Balkinization*, September 21, 2006, balkin.blogspot.com/2006/09/senators-snatch-defeat-from-jaws-of.html.

49   Robert Kuttner, "The John McCain Charade," *Boston Globe*, September 30, 2006, p. A11.

50   Editorial, "Rushing Off a Cliff," *New York Times*, September 28, 2006, p. A22.

51   Bruce Ackerman, "Railroading Injustice," *Los Angeles Times*, September 28, 2006, p. B13.

52   A CBS/*New York Times* poll taken in September 2006 asked, "When it comes to the treatment of prisoners of war, should the United States follow the international agreements that it and other countries have agreed to, or should the U.S. do what it thinks is right, even if other countries disagree?" Sixty-three percent chose following international agreements, while only 32 percent said the U.S. should do what it thinks is right.

Chapter 5

1   *NBC Nightly News*, NBC, March 10, 2004.

2   "Gephardt Promotes McCain Candidacy," *New York Times*, May 26, 2004, p. A16.

3   Sherry Gay Stolberg and Jodi Wilgoren, "Undeterred by McCain Denials, Some See Him as Kerry's No. 2," *New York Times*, May 15, 2004, p. A1.

4   *Meet the Press*, NBC, May 16, 2004.

5   David Ignatius, "The McCain Choice," *Washington Post*, May 21, 2004, p. A25.

6   *Fox News Sunday*, Fox News, March 21, 2004.

7   *Meet the Press*, NBC, April 11, 2004.

8   Sherry Gay Stolberg and Jodi Wilgoren, "Undeterred by McCain Denials, Some See Him as Kerry's No. 2," *New York Times*, May 15, 2004, p. A1.

9   David M. Halbfinger, "McCain Is Said to Tell Kerry He Won't Join," *New York Times*, June 12, 2004, p. A1.

10 Bob Cusack, "Democrats Say McCain Nearly Abandoned GOP," *Hill*, March 29, 2007, p. 1.

11 Jonathan Chait, "This Man Is Not a Republican," *New Republic*, January 31, 2000, p. 26.

12 Jonathan Chait, "What's in a Name?" *New Republic*, April 29, 2002, p. 16.

13 Donald Lambro, "Rift on Right Over Vietnam Reduces Risks for President," July 12, 1995, p. A1.

14 Matt Bai, "McCain's 'Mooseketeers,'" *Newsweek*, July 30, 2001, p. 31.

15 Jonathan Chait, "What's in a Name?" *New Republic*, April 29, 2002, p. 16.

16 John Judis, "Neo-McCain," *New Republic*, October 16, 2006, p. 15.

17 James Traub, "The Submerging Republican Majority," *New York Times Magazine*, June 18, 2006, p. 30.

18 Richard Wolffe, "McCain's Right Flank," *Newsweek*, May 22, 2006, p. 34.

19 William Safire, "The Deciding Voter," *New York Times*, September 1, 2004, p. A19.

20 Jacob Weisberg, "The Closet McCain," *Slate*, April 12, 2006.

21 Ralph Nader, "John McCain: The Maverick Gunning for the Oval Office," *Time*, May 8, 2006, p. 54.

22 Massimo Calabresi and Perry Bacon Jr., "America's 10 Best Senators," *Time*, April 24, 2006, p. 24.

23 Data on *Congressional Quarterly* party unity scores going back to the thirty-fifth Congress can be found at pooleandrosenthal.com/party_unity.htm.

24 James Kuhnhenn, "Democrats Sense Opportunity in Congress, Announce Agenda," Knight Ridder, April 26, 2005.

25 *The Chris Matthews Show*, Universal TV Talk Productions, April 24, 2005.

26 *Fox News Sunday*, Fox News, February 13, 2005.

27 *Special Report with Brit Hume*, Fox News, March 2, 2005.

28 Even a poll sponsored in August 2002 by the tobacco company Philip Morris found that Americans supported FDA regulation of tobacco by 58 percent to 35 percent.

29 *Meet the Press*, NBC, April 2, 2006.

30 The poll was taken in June 2006; the text of the question was as follows: "One proposal would allow undocumented immigrants who have

been living and working in the United States for a number of years, and who do not have a criminal record, to start on a path to citizenship by registering that they are in the country, paying a fine, getting finger-printed, and learning English, among other requirements. Do you support or oppose this, or haven't you heard enough about it to say?"

31 This poll, taken in June 2006, asked, "Which comes closest to your view about what government policy should be toward illegal immigrants currently residing in the United States? Should the government deport all illegal immigrants back to their home country, allow illegal immigrants to remain in the United States in order to work but only for a limited amount of time, or allow illegal immigrants to remain in the United States and become U.S. citizens but only if they meet certain requirements over a period of time?"

32 Kirk Victor, "McCain's Evolution," *National Journal*, August 8, 2001, p. 2464.

33 ibid.

34 Luiza Savage, "Better Than Bush," *Maclean's*, October 17, 2005, p. 34.

35 South Carolina Republican debate, February 15, 2000, CNN.com, transcripts .cnn.com/TRANSCRIPTS/0002/15/lkl.00.html.

36 Connie Bruck, "McCain's Party," *New Yorker*, May 30, 2005, p. 15.

37 ibid.

38 Jonathan Darman, "The Iraq Primary," *Newsweek*, November 27, 2006, p. 31.

39 *Late Edition with Wolf Blitzer*, CNN, September 29, 2002.

40 *Larry King Live*, CNN, September 24, 2002.

41 Interview with Wolf Blitzer on CNN, January 21, 2003.

42 *Hardball with Chris Matthews*, MSNBC, March 12, 2003.

43 *MSNBC Live*, MSNBC, January 7, 2007.

44 *Larry King Live*, CNN, March 19, 2003.

45 *Today*, NBC, October 11, 2006.

46 *Hannity and Colmes*, Fox News, October 10, 2006. McCain was speaking of his outspoken criticism of the Clinton administration when he said he was "heavily involved in [the issue] at the time."

47 *The Early Show*, CBS, October 11, 2006.

48 Roger Simon, "McCain's Support of War Looms as Barrier to Presidential Hopes," Bloomberg News, April 20, 2006.

49 Richard Cohen, "Two Cities McCain Stands to Lose," *Washington Post*, December 19, 2006, p. A29.

50 *Scarborough Country*, MSNBC, December 5, 2006.

51 *This Week with George Stephanopoulos*, ABC, October 24, 2004.

52 Byron York, "America's (Second) Most Important Hawk," *Hill*, December 8, 2005, p. 16.

53 *Face the Nation*, CBS, September 24, 2006.

54 Andrew Clevenger, "McCain Stumps for Wakim at City Luncheon," *Charleston Gazette*, October 17, 2006.

55 Ari Berman, "The Real McCain," *Nation*, December 12, 2005.
56 congress.cwfa.org.
57 www.cc.org/2004scorecard.pdf.
58 Jonathan Chait, "Strategic Planning," *New Republic* online, April 24, 2006.
59 Charles Mahtesian, "There's No Getting Past His Past," *National Journal*, May 1, 2004, p. 1350.
60 John McCain, *Worth the Fighting For*. New York: Random House: 2003, p. 86.
61 Mark Leibovich, "Pedal to the Metal," *Washington Post*, May 12, 2004, p. C1.
62 Connie Bruck, "McCain's Party," *New Yorker*, May 30, 2005, p. 15.
63 Adam Nagourney, "McCain Emphasizing His Conservative Bona Fides," *New York Times*, April 9, 2006, p. 33.
64 Morris Fiorina, with Samuel J. Abrams and Jeremy C. Pope, *Culture War? The Myth of a Polarized America*. New York: Pearson, Longman, 2004.
65 Jacob S. Hacker and Paul Pierson, *Off Center: The Republican Revolution and the Erosion of American Democracy*. New Haven: Yale University Press, 2005, p. 40.
66 ibid., pp. 28–29.
67 ibid.

Chapter 6

1 Howard Fineman, "Living Politics: McCain's Moment," *Newsweek* Web exclusive, June 22, 2005.
2 Connie Bruck, "McCain's Party," *New Yorker*, May 30, 2005, p. 15.
3 Sebastian Mallaby, "A Time for McCain?" *Washington Post*, October 3, 2005, p. A17.
4 Trudy Rubin, "The McCain Alternative," *Philadelphia Inquirer*, November 17, 2005.
5 E. J. Dionne, "The Maverick as Moralist," *Washington Post*, December 11, 2005, p. T7.
6 Jeffrey Birnbaum, "Results Give Clinton and McCain Food for Thought on the Future," *Washington Post*, November 9, 2006, p. A37.
7 Editorial, "Listen to Arizona; Voters There Backed Supporters of Comprehensive Immigration Reform. Will Washington Follow Their Lead?" *Los Angeles Times*, November 9, 2006, p. A 36.
8 *Morning Edition*, NPR, November 17, 2006.
9 *The Situation Room*, CNN, November 13, 2006.
10 Stephen Dinan, "McCain Gains Political Capital in Elections," *Washington Times*, November 8, 2006, p. A1.
11 *The Situation Room*, CNN, November 15, 2008.
12 Janet Hook, "McCain Moves Toward '08 Presidential Run," *Los Angeles Times*, November 15, 2006, p. A19.

13 Jill Lawrence, "McCain Committee Lays Groundwork for '08 Bid," *USA Today*, November 15, 2006, p. 7A.

14 Linda Feldman, "Two Years Till Election Day, and the Race Is On," *Christian Science Monitor*, November 15, 2006, p. 1.

15 Jerry Falwell, *The 700 Club*, Christian Broadcasting Network, September 13, 2001.

16 *The NewsHour with Jim Lehrer*, PBS, February 28, 2000.

17 Adam Nagourney, "McCain Emphasizing His Conservative Bona Fides," *New York Times*, April 9, 2006, p. 33A.

18 *Meet the Press*, NBC, April 2, 2006.

19 Wayne Slater, "Ties with the Right Touted," *Dallas Morning News*, January 6, 2007.

20 Hagee lays out these predictions in his book *Jerusalem Countdown* (Frontline, 2006). See Sarah Posner, "Pastor Strangelove," *American Prospect*, June 6, 2006.

21 Teddy Davis, "McCain Woos the Right, Makes Peace with Falwell," ABCNEWS.com, March 28, 2006, abcnews.go.com/Politics/print?id= 1779141.

22 *The Early Show*, CBS, January 25, 2006.

23 Carla Marinucci, "McCain Gets Boost from Bush's Troubles," *San Francisco Chronicle*, August 20, 1999, p. A3.

24 *Late Edition with Wolf Blitzer*, CNN, August 22, 1999.

25 Ron Fournier, "McCain Clashes with Anti-Abortion Group over Comments," Associated Press, August 24, 1999.

26 ibid.

27 *Hotline* National Briefing, February 28, 2006, nationaljournal.com/about/ hotline/webads.html.

28 Teddy Davis, "McCain Woos the Right, Makes Peace with Falwell," ABCNEWS.com, March 28, 2006, abcnews.go.com/Politics/print?id= 1779141.

29 *This Week*, ABC, November 19, 2006.

30 "McCain: Roe v. Wade Should Be Overturned," Associated Press, February 19, 2007.

31 "Matthews, Tucker, and Borger Mischaracterized Democrats' History on Abortion," Media Matters for America, December 13, 2005, mediamat ters.org/items/200512130003.

32 "Matthews Accused Sen. Clinton of Taking 'Poll-Tested Path' and 'Trying to Play It Safe' on Abortion," Media Matters for America, April 24, 2006, mediamatters.org/items/200604240010.

33 "McCain: Same-Sex Marriage Ban Is Un-Republican," CNN.com, July 14, 2004, www.cnn.com/2004/ALLPOLITICS/07/14/mccain.marriage/.

34 *This Week with George Stephanopoulos*, ABC, November 19, 2006.

35 Teddy Davis, "McCain Woos the Right, Makes Peace with Falwell," ABC
    News.com, March 28, 2006, abcnews.go.com/Politics/print? id=1779141.
36 Elisabeth Bumiller, "Bush Remarks Roil Debate over Teaching of Evolu-
    tion," *New York Times*, August 3, 2005, p. A14.
37 "Sen. John McCain on Teaching Intelligent Design in the Classroom," video
    on *Arizona Daily Star* Web site, August 24, 2005.
38 American Association for the Advancement of Science Board of
    Directors, "AAAS Board Resolution on Intelligent Design Theory,"
    press release, October 18, 2002, www.aaas.org/news/releases/2002/
    1106id2.shtml.
39 John Birger, "McCain's Farm Flip," *Fortune*, November 13, 2006, p. 65.
40 ibid.
41 Ron Fournier, "McCain's Straight-Talking Image Called into Question,"
    Associated Press, April 5, 2006.
42 Adam Nagourney, "McCain Emphasizing His Conservative Bona Fides,"
    New York Times, April 9, 2006, p. A33.
43 Paul Krugman, "The Right's Man," *New York Times*, March 13, 2006, p. 21.
44 "The Note," ABCNews.com, March 13, 2006.
45 E. J. Dionne, "A Maverick No More?" *Washington Post*, March 28, 2006,
    p. A23.
46 *The Daily Show with Jon Stewart*, Comedy Central, April 4, 2006.
47 *Hardball with Chris Matthews*, MSNBC, May 10, 2006.
48 *The Chris Matthews Show*, Universal TV Talk Productions, September 10,
    2006.
49 ibid., November 19, 2006.
50 *Hardball with Chris Matthews*, MSNBC, January 22, 2007.
51 *The Chris Matthews Show*, Universal TV Talk Productions, April 15, 2007.
52 *Hardball with Chris Matthews*, MSNBC, March 14, 2006.
53 ibid., 5:00 p.m. edition, MSNBC, March 10, 2006.
54 ibid., MSNBC, March 14, 2006.
55 ibid., 7:00 p.m. edition, MSNBC, March 10, 2006.
56 ibid.
57 John McCain, Remarks at the Southern Republican Leadership Conference,
    March 10, 2006, www.gwu.edu/~action/2008/mccain031006spt.html.
58 *Hardball with Chris Matthews*, MSNBC, March 13, 2006.
59 *Today*, NBC, March 28, 2007.
60 *Good Morning America*, ABC, April 5, 2006.
61 Massimo Calabresi and Perry Bacon Jr., "America's 10 Best Senators," *Time*,
    April 24, 2006.
62 Carl Hulse, "Foe of Earmarks Has Pet Cause of His Own," *New York Times*,
    February 18, 2006, p. A2.
63 Paul Kane, "McCain Won't Target Members," *Roll Call*, March 10, 2005.

64 Howard Fineman, "Winners and Losers in the Abramoff Scandal," MSNBC.com, January 4, 2006.

65 Alexander Bolton, "Eyeing '08, Sen. McCain Courts K St.," *Hill*, March 8, 2006.

66 Walter V. Robinson, "In Arizona, McCain's Tactics Seen as Power Plays," *Boston Globe*, December 13, 1999, p. A1.

67 *CBS Evening News*, CBS, February 6, 2006.

68 *Lou Dobbs Tonight*, CNN, February 7, 2006.

69 *Hardball with Chris Matthews*, MSNBC, February 7, 2006.

70 Mark Schmitt, "Big Bad John," *American Prospect*, April 8, 2006, p. 8.

71 *Hardball with Chris Matthews*, MSNBC, October 18, 2006.

72 David Broder, "Voters' Authentic Yearning," *Washington Post*, May 11, 2006, p. A27. When McCain and thirteen other senators known as the "Gang of fourteen" brokered a deal to avoid the use of the "nuclear option," eliminating filibusters in the Senate, Broder wrote that the incident "certified McCain as the real leader" of the Senate. Seemingly straining to find an excuse to talk about McCain's time as a prisoner of war, Broder wrote, "The success of the 'Gang of 14' was a rare and welcome triumph over the antagonisms that have been so deeply rooted in the political generation that came of age in the 1960s and 1970s, when the nation was torn by conflicts over civil rights, women's rights, abortion and, most of all, Vietnam. McCain himself served in Vietnam and endured 5½ years of captivity and torture in a Hanoi prison camp." David Broder, "The Senate's Real Leader," *Washington Post*, May 25, 2005, p. A27

73 David Broder, "The McCain Phenomenon," *Washington Post*, August 31, 2004, p. A21.

74 *Glenn Beck*, CNN Headline News, January 3, 2007.

75 Jonathan Chait, "Fake Right," *New Republic*, April 18, 2006.

76 ibid., "McCain Goes Over to the Dark Side," *Los Angeles Times*, March 10, 2007, p. A21.

77 Jacob Weisberg, "The Closet McCain," *Slate*, April 12, 2006.

78 John Judis, "Neo-McCain," *New Republic*, October 16, 2006, pp. 15–21.

79 Jacob Weisberg, "The Closet McCain," *Slate*, April 12, 2006.

80 Eleanor Clift, "Yesterday's Issue," MSNBC.com, November 24, 2006.

81 David Ignatius, "A Man Who Won't Sell His Soul," *Washington Post*, May 3, 2006, p. A23.

82 Todd Purdum, "Prisoner of Conscience," *Vanity Fair*, February 2007.

83 Massimo Calabresi and Perry Bacon Jr., "America's 10 Best Senators," *Time*, April 24, 2006, p. 24.

84 "If It's Sunday, It's Conservative," Media Matters for America, February 14, 2006, pp. 11–13, mediamatters.org/items/200602140002.

85 Mickey Kaus, "Kausfiles," *Slate*, November 22, 2005.

86 "The Note," ABCNews.com, March 7, 2006.

87 Allan Wolper and Greg Mitchell, *Editor & Publisher*, January 31, 2000, p. 18.

88 *The Chris Matthews Show*, Universal TV Talk Productions, September 10, 2006.

89 *CBS Evening News*, CBS, February 5, 2000.

90 Mike Allen, "McCain Vows Democratic Outreach," *Politico*, April 28, 2007.

91 Michael Cooper, "McCain Tries to Recapture Vigor of His Last Campaign," *New York Times*, April 29, 2007.

Postscript

1 *Hardball with Chris Matthews*, MSNBC, January 2, 2008.

2 Chuck Todd, "Get Your Post-Caucus Spin Now," MSNBC.com, January 2, 2008.

3 *Hardball with Chris Matthews*, MSNBC, January 2, 2008.

4 ibid.

5 Fox News Channel, January 3, 2008.

6 ibid.

7 MSNBC, January 3, 2008.

8 Jon Meacham, "Giving Principle a Try," *Newsweek* Web exclusive, January 2, 2008.

9 MSNBC, January 8, 2008.

10 CNN, January 11, 2008.

11 John Harris and Jim VandeHei, "Why Reporters Get it Wrong," *Politico*, January, 9, 2008.

Acknowledgments

This book benefited from the contributions of many people at the Media Matters Action Network, most particularly Elbert Ventura and Robert Savillo, without whom the book would not have been possible. Additional assistance was provided by Jamison Foser, Marcia Kuntz, Eric Burns, and Amanda Fazzone. Will Lippincott's guidance and wisdom were invaluable. Finally, the authors wish to thank Andrew Miller and the extraordinary editorial, production, and publicity teams at Vintage/Anchor.